Recipes for Dairy-Free Living

Recipes for
Dairy-Free
Living

Denise Jardine

photography by Caroline Kopp

Celestial Arts
Berkeley • Toronto

Celestial Arts
P.O. Box 7123
Berkeley, California 94707
www.tenspeed.com

Distributed in Australia by Simon and Schuster Australia, in Canada by Ten Speed
Press Canada, in New Zealand by Southern Publishers Group, in South Africa by Real
Books, in Southeast Asia by Berkeley Books, and in the United Kingdom and Europe by
Airlift Book Company.

Disclaimer: It is not the intent of the author to diagnose or prescribe, nor is it the pur-
pose of this book to replace the services of a health professional. It is advisable to seek
the advice of a licensed, professional health-care provider for any condition that may
require medical attention.

For additional dairy-free information, recipes, and author updates log onto
www.dairyfreeliving.com

Cover Design by Toni Tajima
Interior Design by Tasha Hall
Prop Styling by Carol Hacker/Tableprop
Food Styling by Pouké
Food Stylist Assistant, Samantha Campbell

Library of Congress Cataloging-in-Publication Data
Jardine, Denise.
    Recipes for dairy-free living / Denise Jardine.
    p. cm.
    Includes bibliographical references and index.
    ISBN 1-58761-100-7
    1. Milk-free diet—Recipes.   I. Title.
RM234.5.J37 2001
613.2'6—dc21

                                    2001005748

First printing, 2001
Printed in the United States of America

2 3 4 5 6 7 8 9 10 – 05 04 03

Contents

Dedication

This book is dedicated to my parents, Sava and Mary Dragisich, for instilling in me the importance of family, culture, and a love for creating and eating delicious food.

In loving memory of mother, Doris, Baba Popovich, Tete Danie and Uncle J. J. Radovich, Tete Babe and Uncle Joe Reculin, Bobbie and Wayne Kasom, Baba Sophie, and Kuntanka, whose love, inspiration, and guidance transcend time.

Acknowledgments

A heartfelt thank-you goes out to four dynamic women: Katy Schneider, my most excellent friend, artist, and enthusiast; Akiko Shurtleff, accomplished cookbook author and artist, for stepping out on a limb and believing in me; my mother next door, Barbara Ryan, for her humor and insightful musings on the initial text; and Dr. Elizabeth Seet, M.D., for her compassion, and for listening.

I am immensely grateful to my editors, Annie Nelson and Aaron Wehner, for their expertise and hard work and for believing in this project and making it the best it can be. Many thanks to Jorge Chevez, Jonathan Rubin, Marc Rubenstein, Gerard Rodriguez, and Maureen Kellond for their flexibility, enthusiasm, and culinary excellence. Working with each of you is an honor and a pleasure.

More personal thanks are owed to my family and friends for their encouragement and for sharing and critiquing many a dairy-free meal, especially Nick, Dorothy, Adam, Christine, and Stephanie Dragisich; Bruce, Barry, and Marsha Savin; Mark Reculin; Monte and Stana Anselmo; Bill, Richard, Susan, and Kirsten Jardine; Rose, Fred, and Fred Jr. Baumer; Andrea and Rick Arbore; Jack and Dolly Hendrickson; Derek and Leslie Floreani; Paul and Lesa Martin; Jim and Mary Fritz; Matt and Jody Friedman; Suzanne and Tom Allen; Linda Brock; Brad Baker; Andrea Shilich; and Janine Grupalo.

Finally, I must express loving gratitude to my husband, Robert, a fabulous cook in his own right, for serving as manuscript and recipe consultant, and dedicated taste tester, and for working so hard to support me in every sense of the word. Without him, this book would not have been possible. I love you.

Preface

I was a dairy-aholic. I craved it, I had to have it! Often I would wake up in the middle of the night craving a glass of milk. Coming home from work, I looked forward to cheese and crackers. In addition to a glass of milk at dinner, the meal itself always had an element of dairy in it: perhaps crumbled cheese on a salad, a baked potato with butter and sour cream, cheesy lasagna, or a scoop of rich ice cream for dessert. Dining out was always a pleasure, as the menu would have an assortment of entrées to choose from containing dairy in one form or another, not to mention dessert with a latte. I couldn't get enough dairy, and the interesting thing is, I had no idea it was making me sick.

Over the years, I suffered from an assortment of gastrointestinal ailments. My symptoms included bloating, constipation, and even intestinal bleeding. I saw more doctors and endured more tests than I care to remember. My doctors genuinely wanted to help me but didn't know how, and their approach was always to treat the symptoms. Their diagnoses varied over the years from psychosomatic illness to stress to possible cancer! At one point I was told that if I became pregnant I should expect the symptoms to get worse because they were thought to be hormonal. In the meantime, my symptoms continued to escalate. I was caught in a downward spiral.

I discovered my lactose intolerance quite by accident. My medical insurance was about to change, and I had to find a new doctor. I began the process of getting recommendations, found a doctor, and made my appointment. At some point during my exam I burst into tears and told my new doctor about my long, sordid medical past. She took the time to listen to my story and made dietary recommendations that made sense. When I left that day, I started on an elimination food diet, coupled with a daily food diary. At the end of the exercise it was clear beyond a doubt that I had a dairy allergy that had gone undiagnosed for approximately eighteen years.

What's a dairy-aholic to do when dairy is no longer an option? The horror set in once I realized all of the dairy-rich foods I would be giving up. How could I live without milk, cheese, yogurt, and ice cream? At the same time, I was relieved to have finally discovered the cause of my symptoms and discomfort. I began reading everything I could get my hands on pertaining to the subject. Now that dairy was no longer going to be part of my life, I was presented with a whole new set of challenges. How was I going to get the proper amount of calcium in my diet? I couldn't imagine cooking without dairy; how would my sauces and soups be creamy, my desserts satisfying? Entertaining was critical to me, but how could I subject my family and friends to nondairy meals?

I'll show you the answers I found to all these and many other questions in the chapters that follow. For those who wish to learn more, I've listed additional resources and agencies on page 178. The enjoyment of food is one of life's great pleasures. It is my hope that this book will help the millions of people who have decided to give up dairy products out of necessity or by personal choice. These delicious and innovative recipes will allow you to experience how satisfying dairy-free cooking can be.

Introduction

I am fortunate to have grown up with a rich Slavic heritage in an environment where gathering in love with family and friends was closely intertwined with food. My earliest and fondest memories are of my grandmother's kitchen, being cradled by the warmth and wonderful aromas, the buzz of conversation and laughter filling the air. As a young girl, I would watch my grandmother stretch strudel dough on the kitchen table or wait for freshly caught mountain trout to dry in my uncle's smokehouse. Enjoying simple and down-to-earth food has always been the mainstay of my family life. Whether the cook was my mother, my grandmother, or one of my aunts, the food was always delicious and the time we spent together both enriching and memorable.

The influence my family has had on my cooking style is immeasurable. My mother's ease at entertaining is amazing, and throwing a party for twenty is second nature for her. She started me in the kitchen early, teaching me what her mother taught her, along with her own style and innovations. My uncle has inspired my gardening practices. He believed in planting only things that could be eaten and had the most fabulous organic garden one could imagine. He taught me how to pick the freshest fruits, vegetables, and herbs from the garden and to use them in simple ways, letting nothing go to waste.

Today my own organic garden provides an abundance of herbs, vegetables, and fruit throughout the year and has inspired many recipes. However, the challenge now lies in re-creating many of my favorites without using dairy products. Although it's not an easy task, it's ultimately a rewarding one. Living dairy-free means learning how to identify foods that contain dairy products, discovering dairy-free alternatives that satisfy your cravings, learning about the vast variety of calcium sources, and feeling confident when entertaining that you can prepare satisfying, delectable, dairy-free foods that everyone will enjoy.

Recipes for Dairy-Free Living provides the basic information you need to manage your dairy-free decision and offers a collection of delicious recipes—prepared with accessible ingredients—that will make implementing a dairy-free diet effortless.

Understanding Dairy Components and Problems

Dairy products come in many forms and are in more foods than you might realize. I had no idea how entrenched dairy products are in our culture, nor did I expect to find them in so many everyday foods. Beyond the obvious items in the dairy case, many other products contain dairy in the form of lactose or milk proteins. One example is a dairy protein called casein found in certain brands of tuna fish and soy cheese. In addition to being found in various food items, dairy components are also used in pharmaceutical drugs sold both over the counter and by prescription. So the first step in implementing a dairy-free lifestyle is to have a basic understanding of what dairy is and how it can affect us.

Lactose Intolerance

Lactose is milk sugar and occurs naturally in the milk of animals. Many people are sensitive to milk products because they lack the enzyme called lactase. This enzyme, found in the gastrointestinal tract, is critical in the digestion of lactose. If the lactase enzyme is missing or depleted, the gastrointestinal tract cannot adequately break down the milk sugar, leading to a wide variety of symptoms. Individuals experiencing this are described as being "lactose intolerant."

The symptoms of lactose intolerance can vary greatly from one individual to the next as well as varying within the individual. They include but are not limited to stomach cramps, bloating, flatulence, and diarrhea. It's difficult to estimate how many people are lactose intolerant. Because the condition encompasses so many ethnic groups, it is estimated that up to 50 million Americans suffer from some form of dairy intolerance. In addition to ethnic origins, age plays a major role in the ability to tolerate dairy products. As we mature, the lactase in our gastrointestinal tract begins to diminish. That is why lactose intolerance can intensify with age.

Each individual's tolerance is dependent upon the amount of lactase in his or her system and the amount of dairy products ingested at any given time. Think of it this way: If you have a limited amount of lactase enzyme in your gastrointestinal tract and you ingest limited amounts of dairy, your body may be able to break the lactose down on its own. However, if you have a limited amount of lactase enzyme available and you ingest moderate to high amounts of dairy, you will have exceeded your body's capacity to digest the lactose and thus will experience symptoms.

Unfortunately, there is no way to establish what constitutes limited, moderate, and high dairy intake, because it is completely individualized. To some people, limited amounts of dairy can translate to milk on their cereal in the morning, yogurt in the afternoon, and pasta with Parmesan cheese for dinner. For others this amount of dairy would be considered high or excessive. And some people could tolerate this amount of dairy only if they avoided dairy products entirely for the next day or two.

Many people who are strictly lactose intolerant can avoid problems simply by taking a dairy digestive aid. These digestive aids are widely available and can be purchased over the counter at supermarkets, drugstores, and specialty stores. The amount of lactase enzyme you will require will depend on how much dairy you ingest and how much lactase is already present in your gastrointestinal tract. Select a product that has the right amount of FCC lactase units to complement your digestive tract. For example, when comparing various products I found that the suggested dosage could vary drastically from one product to the next, with one brand containing 9,000 FCC lactase units per caplet and another containing only 1,000.

Sensitivity to Milk Proteins

Milk proteins come in many different forms, several with names that are difficult to pronounce. The important thing is to be able to recognize them when they appear on a label. Look for hydrolysates, casein, caseinates, and whey, lactalbumin, and lactoglobulin. All of these are milk proteins.

As with the symptoms of lactose intolerance, reactions to milk proteins can vary greatly from one individual to the next. Sensitivity to milk proteins is generally regarded as a dairy allergy. However, it is possible to be both lactose intolerant and develop a sensitivity to dairy proteins. Symptoms of dairy allergy tend to range in severity from stomach cramps, bloating, flatulence, diarrhea, and constipation to asthma, nasal congestion, skin rash, hives, eczema, mucous buildup, bleeding from the bowel, rectal fissures, and itching. If you suspect that you may have a dairy allergy, seek out a competent food allergist who can help you understand and manage your allergy. Listed in the bibliography are excellent resources for finding an allergist in your area and obtaining additional information.

The Need for Calcium

It's true that dairy products are an important source of calcium. Therefore, when dairy is no longer an option in our diet, we need to find alternative ways to fulfill our daily calcium requirement. Calcium is found in several different food groups, including fruits, vegetables, legumes, grains, poultry, fish, nuts, and seeds. I was quite surprised to find how many calcium-rich foods I was already eating as part of my normal diet. But the question remained, was I getting enough calcium?

To be sure that I would get the calcium my body needed, my doctor recommended that I take a supplement containing 1,200 milligrams of calcium and a multivitamin each day. She emphasized the need to get as much calcium from my diet as possible and that the supplements were simply an insurance policy. Daily calcium requirements vary; it is best to check with your doctor to be sure you're getting enough.

Once you understand the role calcium plays in your overall health and you know which foods are high in calcium, making an informed decision as to how you will meet your daily calcium requirement becomes a lot easier. To find out more, I turned to Kazuko Aoyagi, an expert on the subject of diet, nutrition, and exercise.

Calcium 101
by Kazuko Aoyagi

Most people know that calcium is a mineral necessary for forming and maintaining healthy bones and teeth. However, few people realize that calcium also plays an important role in regulating other body functions, including

- Blood clotting
- Blood pressure

- Enzyme activation
- Contraction and relaxation of muscles (including normal heartbeats)
- Nerve transmission
- Cell membrane permeability (allowing fluids and other materials to pass in and out of cells)

About 98 percent of the calcium in our body is stored in our bones. When there is not enough calcium present in the diet, calcium is "borrowed" from the bones and released into the bloodstream to maintain these essential body functions. Symptoms of calcium deficiency include osteoporosis, rickets, and impaired muscle contraction (muscle cramps). Over time, dietary calcium deficiency can lead to a loss of bone density, resulting in osteoporosis. However, there is still much debate over whether a lack of dietary calcium is the main cause of loss of bone density. Although dairy foods are often touted as a way to build strong bones, there has never been a study that conclusively links the consumption of dairy products to bone health.

Factors Contributing to Healthy Bones

Osteoporosis, or the thinning of the bones, is often associated with older people, but the process can start earlier than you might expect. Peak bone mass is achieved by age twenty-five, so it is important to build strong bones as a youth. After age twenty-five, bone mass replenishment slows, and maintaining bone mass becomes increasingly important. Once bones begin to thin, it is hard to reverse the trend with calcium alone. Many factors, such as diet, exercise, medications, hormones, heredity, and lifestyle choices, can influence both the development of bone density and the ability to maintain bone density during the aging process.

Diet. Bones require a wide variety of nutrients to develop normally and to maintain density after maturity. Simply getting the recommended dietary allowance (RDA) of calcium is not enough to keep your bones healthy. Vitamins and minerals, along with proper nutrition, all play a major role. The key nutrients include protein, calcium, phosphorus, magnesium, zinc, boron, manganese, copper, vitamin D, vitamin C, and vitamin K.

Magnesium is especially important, as it is necessary for transporting calcium to the bones. Consuming gallons of milk or taking hundreds of calcium pills will do no good without the presence of magnesium and other elements and minerals. Ironically, drinking too much milk or taking a large dose of calcium supplements can actually cause a calcium imbalance because milk does not contain enough magnesium.

Calcium Absorption. Calcium balance in adults is complex because your body does not absorb all of the calcium you ingest. When you meet the RDA of 800 milligrams, your body absorbs only 300 milligrams and simply excretes the rest. Phytates found in grains and oxalates found in green leafy vegetables reduce the body's calcium absorption somewhat by binding to calcium so that it cannot be absorbed efficiently. However, recent studies have shown that the amount of fiber, phytates, and oxalates found in the average American diet do not appear to pose a problem for calcium absorption. Research also revealed that vegetarian diets provide adequate amounts of calcium, as measured by body stores.

Exercise. Weight-bearing exercise stimulates bone formation and helps build and maintain strong bones. Thin bones become a major problem when muscles weaken significantly and when bones aren't challenged with weight. A study conducted by NASA showed that weightlessness in space decreased skeletal density in humans and primates by as much as 10 percent. Unfortunately, as we age, most of us become less physically active and the amount of weight-bearing exercise in our daily routine diminishes.

Medications and Hormones. Some medications can actually inhibit the amount of calcium absorbed from food by increasing the calcium lost through the kidneys. One example is a commonly used asthma medication containing corticosteroids. Corticosteroids may also interfere with the production of sex hormones in both men and women, which can contribute to bone density loss as well. The level of gonadal hormones (estrogen for women and testosterone for men) also appears to regulate bone mass by influencing the absorption of calcium in the intestines. If you are taking medications, you should discuss your nutritional concerns with your doctor.

Heredity and Lifestyle. Lactase deficiency is particularly common among North American African Americans, Asians, Mexicans, Native Americans, and people of Mediterranean or Hispanic origin. In most people, it appears to be an acquired, rather than inherited, disorder, sometimes beginning after a viral or bacterial infection or other disorder of the gut. Lifestyle choices such as cigarettes, alcohol, and a high sodium intake can also contribute to bone density loss. If you're interested in learning more about calcium and nutrition, see the additional resources listed in the bibliography (page 177).

Kazuko Aoyagi, Ph.D., is an associate director of technology at a pharmaceutical company and an Advanced Study Program Fellow at MIT, where she continues her study in medicine. Dr. Aoyagi writes articles for various publications, including Prevention *magazine,* Impala Racing Team *newsletters, and health and fitness Web sites.*

Dairy Alternatives in the Supermarkets

When I started cooking dairy-free, one of my biggest tests of success was cooking for my family and friends. Would they notice a change? Would they find my desserts rich and satisfying? I began in the health food store by going on a shopping spree, loading up with all kinds of alternative products for milk, butter, cheese, and yogurt. If I was going to make dairy-free meals enjoyable, it was important to find alternatives I liked. I tried cooking and baking with some of these products and soon found out that not all dairy alternatives are created equal. I also realized that I couldn't run to the health food store every time I needed something. So I changed my approach: I began looking very closely at the new products making their way into supermarkets and was pleasantly surprised to find almost all of the alternatives I was seeking.

Recognizing how busy our lives are these days, I've made sure that all of the recipes in this cookbook use ingredients that can be purchased from supermarkets. As much as I love going to health food and specialty stores, more often than not, I have the time to make only one shopping stop for groceries. For that reason, *Recipes For Dairy-Free Living* uses common, easily obtained ingredients. If you have difficulty finding one of the dairy-free products used here, turn to Manufacturers and Distributors on page 179 for a comprehensive guide with phone numbers and e-mail addresses that will allow you to contact the manufacturer directly.

Food Labeling

The labeling used on food products is a very useful tool when you are trying to monitor your lactose levels or trying to eliminate dairy products from your diet completely. But like everything else, ingredient labels can change without notice. It's a good idea to read the label every time you purchase a product. Manufacturers are always making changes to products for a wide variety of reasons, or they may elect to drop a product from their line altogether. It is best not to assume that a product or brand you've bought before will be the same the next time you buy it. If you have a question about a specific product, contact the manufacturer by mail, e-mail, or phone. You can find contact information for many manufacturers and distributors in the list on page 179.

When reading a label, you need to know the dairy buzzwords. If you find any of the following terms listed on a package label, the product contains dairy. Take time to learn the ones you don't know, write them down, and carry the list with you for reference when shopping. Dairy and its derivatives can be found in the most unusual places, including packaged lunch meats, some of which contain sodium caseinate, whey or nonfat dry milk; some brands of margarine; sliced bread; mayonnaise; and potato chips. The most surprising item I've come across containing a dairy derivative is a popular brand of eye cream that contains lactose.

- Milk in any form—milk proteins, milk solids, malted milk, condensed milk, evaporated milk, dry milk, milkfat, whole milk, low-fat milk, nonfat milk, skim milk, 2 percent milk, 1 percent milk, acidophilus milk, cream, half-and-half, goat's milk, sheep's milk, lactose-free milks. Butter, buttermilk, butter fat, butter oil, artificial butter flavor, yogurt, nougat, custard, pudding, sour cream, cheese, cream cheese, cottage cheese, pasteurized cheese, feta cheese, ice cream, ice milk, sherbet, and some brands of margarine.
- Curds, whey, ghee, casein, rennet casein, lactose, lactulose, hydrolysates, lactalbumin, lactoglobulin, and all types of caseinates in the form of calcium, potassium, sodium, magnesium, and ammonium.

With growing public awareness of the issue of lactose intolerance, manufacturers are recognizing a new market segment and are beginning to respond to the demand for lactose-free products. If you are strictly lactose intolerant, this is good news. However, if you have a dairy allergy, lactose-free products won't help and should be avoided. A product label might indicate that it is lactose free and also that it is nondairy or a dairy alternative, leading you to believe that the product does not contain dairy. It still might contain milk proteins, however, which can trigger allergic reactions. Good examples of products labeled nondairy that contain dairy proteins include some brands of coffee creamers, cheese alternatives, and nondairy whipped toppings.

Kosher Symbols

Special codes or symbols located on the front of a package label can also help identify products that contain dairy. These symbols are actually kosher markings that comply with Jewish dietary laws. The FDA does not regulate these symbols, and it is not mandatory that they appear on food labels. However, when they do appear they can be a useful tool.

"D" indicates that the product contains dairy. Note that sometimes a label will list a "D" yet the ingredients list will not indicate the presence of milk.

This can occur for two reasons:

- The product contains natural flavorings from dairy ingredients.
- The equipment was previously used with dairy products and could have residual amounts, making it unsafe for people with dairy allergies.

I found an example of double-duty equipment use when I was purchasing a bag of tortilla chips and noticed that the package had a "D" listed on it. The ingredients clearly stated that no dairy was present, so I called the manufacturer and questioned it. The person I talked with explained that the equipment had previously been used to produce chips containing dairy, and so they used the "D" label as a precaution.

DE stands for dairy equipment. This means that the product was produced using equipment that was also used to manufacture products containing dairy. The "DE" symbol is not being used as often since "D" covers a broader range of possibilities.

Pareve or Parve indicates that the product does not contain either dairy or meat.

K, U, and **OU** indicate that the product has been manufactured in compliance with Jewish dietary standards and laws. These three symbols have nothing to do with whether or not a dairy ingredient has been used in the product.

Milk Alternatives

In today's supermarkets, finding substitutes for milk is getting easier all the time. Manufacturers are offering a wide selection of satisfying milk alternatives by using rice, soy, oats, and almonds. To add to the choices, these nondairy beverages come in plain (also called original or unsweetened) as well as in an array of flavors such as vanilla, chocolate, carob, strawberry, and coffee. Additionally, nondairy milk choices range from nonfat to 1 percent and 2 percent low-fat and come enriched with calcium and vitamins. The benefit of the enriched varieties is that they provide as much calcium and vitamins A and D as milk.

With so many options, your dairy-free milk choice comes down to personal preference and taste. When I cook or want a glass of ice cold milk, I prefer 1 percent Rice Dream Original Enriched. I find the taste to be lighter, with a subtle sweetness, compared to other nondairy beverages.

The recipes in this cookbook were developed using plain calcium-enriched 1 percent rice or soy milk; both work equally well. Do not use any of the flavored milks unless the recipe calls for it. Each time you use rice or soy milk, be sure to shake the container. It's normal for the milk to separate when it settles.

Dairy-free milk substitutes also have the benefit of convenience. I often buy a couple of cases at a time, since the aseptic packaging allows the product to be kept unopened in the pantry for several months. If you check the date stamped on the package and monitor your supply, you will always have milk on hand. Once the container is opened, it will stay fresh for seven to ten days in the refrigerator, just as milk will.

Butter Alternatives

I have tried as many nondairy margarines as I could get my hands on. The two best for all-around cooking are Shedd's Willow Run Soybean Margarine and

Trader Joe's Natural Margarine. The real test with any margarine comes with baking, and I have had excellent results with both of these brands. Both are pareve soybean margarines that also perform well in cooking and, I believe, have the best flavor.

Other margarines are available in the market, most made with various vegetable oils. These margarines work fine in cooking but should not be used when baking. It's important to note that just because a product is called margarine does not mean it is dairy-free. Many margarines contain milk proteins, whey, or buttermilk used as flavor enhancers, so it's important to look for the word "pareve" on the front of the package.

Eggs

A common mistake many people make is thinking that eggs are considered a dairy product. Although they are often found in the dairy section of most supermarkets, eggs are not a dairy product. For the best flavor and nutritional value, look for eggs from free range hens that are produced without the use of antibiotics, hormones, and pesticides.

Yogurt

Dairy-free yogurt has not made its way into the supermarket yet, and for this reason dairy-free yogurts are not used in any of the recipes in this book. However, dairy-free yogurt is available in health food and specialty stores and is offered in a wide assortment of flavors. My favorites include Nancy's Cultured Soy Yogurt and Trader Joe's Soy Yogurt.

Sour Cream

Several sour cream alternatives are available in both supermarkets and health food stores. Although they are lactose free, all contain casein, a milk protein. For this reason, sour cream alternatives are not included in any of the recipes. I have, however, included a Lean Sour Cream recipe (page 123) that is a fantastic sour cream substitute and can be used in Beef Stroganoff (page 90) or atop a baked potato.

Cheese

Several cheese alternatives can be found in the supermarket, usually located in the produce section, in an assortment of varieties. They can be good to use if you are lactose intolerant but can handle milk proteins. However, if you have a dairy allergy, you should avoid these products, as they do contain milk protein in the form of casein.

A wider selection of cheese alternatives, made from soy, rice, or almonds, can be found in health food stores. Many do contain milk proteins, so check the label carefully; the few that are completely dairy-free tend not to melt very well.

Cheese alternatives are an acquired taste, so be prepared to try several different varieties and flavors before you find one you like. Try my Manicotti Florentine (page 78) and Wild Mushroom Lasagna (page 80); I bet you won't even miss the cheese.

Ice Cream

Sorbet is widely available in many supermarkets and comes in several different brands and flavors, including chocolate, lemon, raspberry, and assorted tropical flavors. Health food or specialty stores are still the best bet for a good selection of soy, rice, or almond-based frozen desserts. Turtle Mountain Inc. manufactures my favorite line of nondairy frozen desserts. As part of their Organic Soy Delicious line, they offer two must-try flavors that taste just like dairy ice cream: Chocolate Peanut Butter and Mint Marble Fudge. They also offer an extensive variety in their three other lines, Purely Decadent Soy Delicious, It's Soy Delicious, and Sweet Nothings.

Tofu

Also known as bean curd, tofu can be found in your supermarket's produce section, although some stores have a special meat/dairy alternative section for it. Tofu is produced in silken, soft, medium, firm, and extra-firm textures and in low-fat or light and calcium-enriched varieties.

The most common variety, "cotton"-style tofu, is primarily sold packed in liquid in plastic tubs and needs to be kept refrigerated. Silken-style tofu is often packaged in aseptic boxes, has a silky-smooth appearance and texture, and does not need refrigeration until it is opened. Silken or soft-pressed tofu is best used in smoothies, sauces, dressings, and other recipes that are blended. Medium and firm tofu work best crumbled in casseroles and for cheesecake. The firm and extra-firm types are best suited for stir-fries, grilling, soups, and salads.

Once you have opened a container of tofu, store any that you have left over by immersing it in water in a container with a tight-fitting lid and keeping it in the refrigerator. Change the water daily, and the tofu will keep for about five days.

Organic Products in the Supermarket

Responding to consumer demand, many supermarkets now carry certified organic produce and free-range chicken and eggs. These items may cost a little more, but they are well worth it for several reasons:

- Any chance to cut down on pesticide residue, genetically engineered organisms (GMO), artificial growth hormones, and antibiotics in our food is always beneficial.
- Purchasing these products will let the store know that organic products are important to you and your family. Supermarkets are more likely to expand their selection of these products when they see an increased demand.
- It encourages farmers to preserve the environment by utilizing alternative farming methods that involve enriching the soil through composting, crop rotation, and natural pest control.
- Organic farming conserves our natural resources, promotes better health, and creates a safer working environment for farm workers.

On December 20, 2000, the United States National Organic Standards were finalized. These standards cover all aspects of organic livestock, crop production, organic certification, processing, and marketing. Products that meet these new standards will display an official U.S. Department of Agriculture (USDA) Organic seal, making it easier for consumers to identify organic products. The new seal will begin to appear on products after October 21, 2002.

About the Recipes

Food is a delight for the senses. As you prepare these recipes, observe how the herbs and spices interact with each other and how the flavors blend together. Throughout the book you will find recipes that say, "Taste and correct the seasonings." As a general rule, your seasonings should complement the dish, not overpower it. If you can taste one seasoning as a separate element, you may have used too much. Start with a small amount and build from there. Be patient. You can always add more salt or pepper, tarragon, or vinegar, but you can't undo it once you've added it. It's important to note that many seasonings intensify as they simmer, so take it slow and enjoy the rich aromas as you go.

Whenever possible, I have used calcium-enriched products when preparing the recipes in this book. It's important when living dairy-free to get an adequate amount of calcium, and for this reason I recommend calcium-enriched rice or soy milk, orange juice, and tofu. None of the recipes that follow contain dairy in any form, including lactose or milk proteins. However, they are loaded with flavor, creatively prepared, and delicious.

My goal is to help you learn about the wonderful alternatives to dairy—for yourself or for family members and friends who would benefit from dairy-free cooking. Each recipe carefully re-creates the flavors and textures that dairy products supply, allowing you to satisfy that craving for dairy in a wholesome and flavorful way. With these recipes, you can prepare scrumptious comfort foods as well as innovative holiday menus for your family and friends. I hope that preparing the recipes in the pages that follow will be a true adventure and will add much to your enjoyment in healthful, dairy-free living. Now, let's get started.

Bon appétit and prijatno!

Special Occasion Menus

Celebrating with food and drink is one of life's greatest pleasures. Whether it's an intimate Valentine's Day dinner, a festive Fourth of July party, or a joyful Christmas feast, we all love to indulge ourselves. Whatever the occasion, there is no need to feel restricted by a dairy-free diet. The menus on the pages that follow will help you plan that special event. These menus offer a wide assortment of entertaining options and have been combined in such a way that many of the dishes can be made in advance. So while the food will impress your guests, you can relax and enjoy the party.

Note: When planning a menu for a casual get-together or a formal dinner party, the key to success is organization. I have found that the more you entertain, the easier it becomes, and you develop a rhythm. One thing that has become part of my rhythm is a staging area, a place where I can stash things aside. My staging area is the laundry room; it's out of the way but accessible. In it, I label bowls and platters to be used for each dish, place the appropriate serving utensils with them, and put them aside. This area is also where I can store the dessert if it needs to reach room temperature before serving, or keep a large tray with the coffee and tea service. When you have things ready to go, you're not scrambling at the last minute and instead can relax.

Each of the special-occasion menus in this chapter is complete with planning tips specific to the occasion. So start your invitation list now with the confidence of knowing that each of these menus has been prepared and thoroughly tested. Your guests will never know your feast is dairy-free.

MENU

Baked Oysters (page 34)

Mixed Greens with Citrus and Candied Pecans (page 37)

Seared Scallops in Asparagus Cream (page 64)

Rum Caramel Flan (page 150) with fresh raspberries

Champagne and mineral water

Baguette

Valentine's Day Dinner

This special dinner has everything you will need for a romantic evening: a lovely oyster appetizer, a refreshing salad, an entrée of tender scallops, and a light, simple dessert. Just add firelight, champagne, and love.

Planning Tips

1 week ahead: Plan the table settings. Decide on the linens, silver, stemware, dishes, candles, and centerpiece.

3 days ahead: Create the shopping list. Buy all the groceries except for the oysters, scallops, and bread, and don't forget the firewood. Prepare the candied pecans.

2 days ahead: Clean the lettuce and prepare the salad dressing.

1 day ahead: Make the asparagus cream and the flan. Prepare the oyster filling. Chill the champagne and mineral water.

Valentine's Day: Purchase the scallops, oysters, and bread. Set the table and get the fire ready in the fireplace.

1 hour before dinner: Prepare and marinate the grapefruit, and bring the dressing to room temperature. Slice the bread. Partially cook the pasta until it is half done. Drain, rinse under cold water, and drain again. This will allow you to cook the pasta quickly just before serving.

⌒ **¹/₂ hour before dinner:** Place the champagne on ice at the table, along with the water. Assemble and bake the oysters. Meanwhile, complete the asparagus cream sauce, boil water for the pasta, and sear the scallops.

Easter Supper

Traditionally lamb or ham is served for Easter supper; this menu offers a lighter approach to celebrating the holiday. It starts with a refreshing salad, a main course wrapped as elegant packages, tender potatoes, fragrant leeks, and a sweet and tangy finale. Of course, you could also include spring lamb or ham if you wish.

Planning Tips

⌒ **1 week ahead:** Plan the guest list and the table settings. Decide on the linens, silver, stemware, dishes, centerpiece, and any other Easter decorations.

⌒ **3 days ahead:** Create the shopping list. Buy all the groceries except for the fish and bread.

⌒ **2 days ahead:** Clean the watercress and make the dressing. Chill the wine and beverages.

⌒ **1 day ahead:** Purchase the fish and bread. Assemble the halibut wraps. Steam the leeks. Make the tart, and set the table.

⌒ **Easter Sunday, 2¹/₂ hours before supper:** Assemble the potatoes. Bring the leeks to room temperature, make the filling, and assemble the leeks. Prepare the sauce for the wraps.

⌒ **1 to 1¹/₄ hours before supper:** Following the recipe instructions, bake the potatoes for 30 minutes, decrease the oven temperature, and place the fish in the oven with the potatoes; continue baking. Bring the dressing to room temperature.

⌒ **¹/₂ hour before supper:** Assemble the salad, but do not dress it until ready to serve. Bring the tart to room temperature. Place the rolls in a basket. Open the wine. Broil the leeks. Remove the potatoes and fish from the oven and let rest. Meanwhile, dress and serve the salad.

MENU

Watercress, cucumber, and tomato salad with Creamy Tarragon Dressing (page 42)

Halibut in Swiss Chard Wraps (page 60)

Scalloped Potatoes (page 92)

Lemon Garlic Crusted Leeks (page 103)

Lemon Blueberry Tart (page 142)

White wine and assorted beverages

Assorted dinner rolls

Coffee and tea

If planning an Easter egg hunt, here are a few things to keep in mind:

1. Count and write down the exact number of eggs and treats you will be hiding.
2. Remember the hiding spots.
3. If you have pets, keep them in the house or secured during the hunt.
4. When the hunt is over, count the eggs. Be sure to pick up any remaining eggs or treats. If you don't, your pets are sure to find them, and eating the treats could make them sick.

Mother's Day Brunch

Relaxing under an umbrella, sipping a little bubbly is just what the doctor ordered for Mother's Day. This menu is colorful, elegant, and versatile, and most of it can be prepared in advance. Set the table with Mom's favorite colors, and plan on lots of fresh flowers.

Planning Tips

1 week ahead: Plan the table settings. Decide whether you will be eating inside or out, and choose the linens, flatware, stemware, dishes, and centerpiece.

3 days ahead: Create the shopping list. Buy all the groceries except for the crab.

2 days ahead: Make the orange juice and chill the champagne and water. Roast and clean the red bell peppers and clean the spinach. Make the dressing and clean the butter lettuce.

1 day ahead: Purchase the crab. Bake the bread. Boil the potatoes. If serving indoors, set the table. If not, have everything stacked and ready to go, including flower arrangements.

Mother's Day morning: If serving outdoors, set the table. Clean and slice the fruit. Slice and arrange the bread on a platter, and cover until ready to serve.

1 hour before brunch: Fry the potatoes, and cook the frittata; keep both warm in a 200° oven. Assemble the fruit salad and serve.

Father's Day Brunch

It's Dad's day, a day to take it easy, read the paper, and enjoy a leisurely brunch in the garden. Although this menu looks impressive, it's actually simple to prepare and takes on a Mediterranean theme. In keeping with that theme, make a centerpiece of fresh potted herbs like rosemary, oregano, thyme, and sage, and have lots of small dishes of marinated olives on the table.

Planning Tips

🍃 **1 week ahead:** Plan the table settings. Decide on the linens, flatware, glassware, dishes, and centerpiece.

🍃 **3 days ahead:** Create the shopping list, and buy all the groceries.

🍃 **2 days ahead:** Prepare the ratatouille. Chill the Bloody Mary mix, cut up the celery, and make ice.

🍃 **Father's Day morning:** Set the table. Bake the muffins. Bring the ratatouille to room temperature.

🍃 **1 hour before brunch:** Prepare the tortilla and keep it warm in a 200° oven.

Fourth of July Party

Red, white, and blue are the colors of the day, so build your table decorations around this theme. Vibrant red, white, and golden-yellow flowers arranged in a blue vase add color and beauty to the table, and for festive star-spangled napkins, wrap your silverware up in red-and-white and blue-and-white bandanas, and tie them with ribbon. Consider sausages or hot dogs for the kids, with pocket chicken sandwiches for the adults.

Planning Tips

🍃 **1 week ahead:** Plan the table settings. Decide on the linens, silverware, glassware, dishes, and table decorations. You may want to consider acrylic or plastic for an outdoor gathering.

🍃 **3 days ahead:** Create the shopping list, including sausages or hot dogs, boneless, skinless chicken breast halves (1 per person), pita bread, buns, lettuce, tomato, and assorted condiments. Buy all the groceries. Make the rub.

🍃 **2 days ahead:** Prepare the dressing for the slaw. Make the iced tea, and chill the beer, wine, and beverages.

🍃 **1 day ahead:** Marinate the chicken with the rub. Cover and refrigerate. Make the beans. Prepare the vegetables for the slaw and store them in a large plastic bag in the refrigerator; do not toss with the dressing. Prepare the ice cream mixture, but do not freeze. Prep the ice cream maker by freezing the cylinder if necessary.

↪**The morning of the Fourth:** Set the table. Buy lots of ice. Place the beverages and the ice in an ice chest. Leave one bag of ice in the freezer for backup. Wash the lettuce, slice the tomatoes, and gather any condiments. Keep refrigerated. Cut the pita bread in half to form pockets for the sandwiches, and keep in a plastic bag until ready to grill and assemble.

↪**3 hours before serving:** Assemble the slaw. Bake the corn bread. Heat the beans and prepare the berries for the dessert by tossing 1 cup blueberries and 2 cups hulled and sliced strawberries in a bowl with 1 teaspoon of sugar. Cover and refrigerate.

↪**$1/2$ hour before serving:** Fire up the barbecue (350°, a medium-hot fire), allow an additional half-hour if using coals. Grill the chicken until the juices run clear, 8 to 10 minutes. Grill the sausages or hot dogs according to the package directions.

↪**$1/2$ hour before dessert:** Churn the coconut ice cream. Spoon it into bowls and top with the berries.

Autumn Vegan Supper

If you have vegan guests coming for dinner, and you have never entertained vegan before, it can be a little intimidating. Here is a menu that is entirely free of animal products and is absolutely delicious. The hearty quality of this menu honors the flavors of the season with a creamy cabbage soup, a satisfying entrée, bright root vegetable mashed potatoes, the best creamed spinach I have ever tasted, and a tender apple tart to finish the meal.

Planning Tips

↪**1 week ahead:** Plan the table settings. Decide on the linens, silverware, glassware, dishes, and table decorations.

↪**3 days ahead:** Create the shopping list and buy all the groceries.

↪**2 days ahead:** Prepare the marinade and marinate the tofu. Chill the white wine and water.

MENU

Cabbage Bisque (page 54) made with Vegetable Stock (page 165)

Pan-Seared Tofu (page 106)

Sweet Potato–Parsnip Mash (page 94)

Creamed Spinach (page 102)

Spiced Apple Tart (page 146)

Red and white wine and mineral water

Coffee and herbal tea

1 day ahead: Prepare the soup. Clean and chop the spinach. Make the sauce for the spinach. Prepare and bake the tart. Set the table.

1 hour before guests arrive: Chop the onion for the spinach, place in a small bowl, cover, and set aside. Boil the potatoes and keep warm. Bring the sauce for the spinach and the soup to room temperature.

1/2 hour before serving: Assemble the spinach. Mash the potatoes.

15 minutes before serving: Sear the tofu and reduce the sauce. Rewarm the soup, spinach, and potatoes. Serve.

Thanksgiving Dinner

If you're in charge of making the Thanksgiving dinner this year, this simple menu is one that you can easily add to, subtract from, or modify to suit your needs. Select appetizers that are light, the kind that can be nibbled on through the course of the afternoon, making sure everyone has room for the scrumptious meal and a slice of pumpkin cheesecake.

Planning Tips

1 to 2 weeks ahead: Order a fresh, organic turkey. Decide on the linens, silver, stemware, dishes, centerpiece, and any other Thanksgiving decorations. Purchase the wine, liquor, and assorted beverages.

3 days ahead: Create the shopping list and buy all the groceries except for the turkey, rolls, and ice. Organize the refrigerator, making necessary space. Prepare the cranberry sauce. Bake and toast the corn bread for the stuffing. Roast the chestnuts.

2 days ahead: Prepare the soup. Set the table. Organize platters, bowls, and serving utensils.

1 day ahead: Pick up the turkey, rolls, and ice. Prepare the stuffing, but do not do the final assembly. Prepare the turkey stock for the gravy. Prepare the cheesecake; cover and refrigerate. Steam the brussels sprouts. Organize predinner drinks, coffee, and tea service. Create a list noting when each dish needs to begin cooking.

Thanksgiving morning: Peel the potatoes and set them aside in cold water. Finish the stuffing. Prepare the turkey for roasting and set aside.

⏀**5 hours before dinner:** Preheat the oven for 20 minutes before placing the turkey in it. Prepare the Soy Velvet Whipped Cream.

⏀**1 to 2 hours before dinner:** Bring the soup to room temperature. Place the cranberry sauce on the table. Cook the potatoes. Sauté the shallots. Put the extra stuffing in the oven 1 hour before serving. Bring the cheesecake to room temperature.

⏀**30 minutes before dinner:** Remove the turkey from the oven, cover with aluminum foil, and let rest. Meanwhile, make the gravy and heat the soup. Assemble the brussels sprouts. Mash the potatoes. Serve the first course.

Christmas Eve Dinner

I grew up in a house with many traditions. One of them was that on Christmas Eve we always sat down to a delicious and peaceful seafood dinner. I guess my mother wanted a moment of calm before the deluge of gifts and the arrival of the twenty or so relatives and friends the next day. The salad is simple, the stew is rich in color and texture yet easy to prepare, and the dessert is in keeping with the season.

Planning Tips

⏀**2 days ahead:** Plan the table settings. Keep it simple but festive. Bake the cookies, if you have not already made them as part of the cookie platter for Christmas Day.

⏀**1 day ahead:** Create the shopping list; include a mixture of colorful salad greens and 1 fresh pomegranate. Buy all the groceries. Clean the lettuce, seed the pomegranate, and make the dressing. Prepare the ice cream mixture, but do not freeze. Prep the ice cream maker by freezing the cylinder if necessary.

⏀**Christmas Eve, 45 minutes before dinner:** Prepare the stew.

⏀**10 minutes before serving:** Slice the bread. Toss the greens and dressing together, sprinkle with pomegranate seeds.

⏀**1/2 hour before dessert:** Churn the ice cream and serve it with the cookies.

MENU

Tossed greens and pomegranate seeds with oil and vinegar dressing

Coconut-Lime Seafood Stew (page 58)

Soy Nog Ice Cream (page 160) with Ginger Cookies (page 158)

White wine

Crusty French bread

Christmas Dinner

During this busiest of seasonings, presenting an elegant Christmas dinner for family and friends doesn't have to be difficult. This collection of recipes offers a festive, colorful menu that's not only brimming with superb flavor but is also visually appealing. Keep the appetizers simple by offering tasty bites such as fresh prawns with cocktail sauce, Swiss Chard and Almond Torta (page 28), tapenades, marinated olives, and Mediterranean Ratatouille (page 24) with a basket of assorted toasted breads (page 173) and crackers.

Planning Tips

◯ **2 to 3 weeks ahead:** Make the cookies and freeze them. Plan the guest list. Decide on the linens, silver, stemware, dishes, centerpiece, and any other Christmas decorations.

◯ **1 week ahead:** Order the fish. Purchase the wine, liquor, and assorted beverages.

◯ **2 days ahead:** Create the shopping list and buy all the groceries except for the fish, bread, and ice. Organize the refrigerator, making necessary space. Prepare the dressing for the salad and clean the spinach. Make the soup. Prepare and freeze the sorrel butter molds.

◯ **1 day ahead:** Purchase the fish, bread, and ice. Roast the beets. Make the filling for the salmon and the sauce. Prepare the chocolate almond cake; cover and keep at room temperature. Organize the predinner drinks, coffee, and tea service. Create a list noting when each dish needs to begin cooking.

◯ **Christmas morning:** Assemble the salmon in the pastry, cover, and refrigerate. Peel the beets, cover, and set aside.

◯ **1 hour before dinner:** Prepare the pilaf. Set out the dessert. Preheat the oven. Put water on to boil and steam the asparagus spears for 5 to 7 minutes; keep warm. Put the bread on the table. Remove the salmon from the refrigerator. Keep covered.

◯ **30 minutes before dinner:** Heat the soup. Toss and assemble the salad. Place the salmon in the oven. Serve the soup, then the salad. By the time the first course is finished, the salmon will be done. Serve the salmon, rice pilaf, and asparagus topped with the sorrel butter.

MENU

Carrot and Roasted Red Pepper Soup (page 46)

Spinach, Pear, and Beet Salad with Sherry Dressing (page 36)

Salmon in Puff Pastry (page 56)

Wild Lemon Pilaf with Currants (page 97)

Asparagus with Sorrel Herb Butter (page 123)

Flourless Chocolate Almond Cake (page 139)

Assorted cookie platter— Holiday Marzipan Cookies (page 161), Oatmeal Almond Lace Cookies (page 159), Ginger Cookies (page 158), Tea Cakes (page 156), Bird's Nest Cookies (page 157), and Chocolate Mint Cookies (page 152)

Coffee and tea

Predinner cocktails, wine with dinner, and assorted beverages

Assorted purchased breads

Holiday Cocktail Party for Twenty

Start with a purchased ham, bread, and assorted mustards, and then build the buffet around them by offering an abundance of sophisticated and delicious dishes, doubling the recipes as needed. As a rule of thumb, consider serving about seven to eight different items per twenty people. For every ten additional people, add one more item. Set up the buffet by placing the plates and napkins at the beginning, then stagger and elevate some of the dishes in the back to create visual interest. Set the dessert, coffee, and tea service on a separate table.

Planning Tips

⤵**3 to 4 weeks ahead:** Plan the guest list and send out the invitations.

⤵**1 to 2 weeks ahead:** Decide on the linens, dishes, flowers, and any other holiday decorations, and plan the table layout. Purchase the wine, liquor, mixes, assorted beverages, and garnishes.

⤵**3 days ahead:** Create the shopping list and buy all the groceries except for the salmon, shrimp, rolls, and ice. Organize the refrigerator, making necessary space. Prepare the caramelized balsamic onions, the herb toasts, and the pita crisps.

⤵**2 days ahead:** Prepare the eggplant spread. Marinate the chicken skewers.

⤵**1 day ahead:** Purchase the fish and rolls. Assemble the salmon cakes. Cover and refrigerate. Prepare the potatoes and clean the endive. Make the fruit tartlets. Prepare the cocktail garnishes.

⤵**Morning of the party:** Purchase the ice for ice chests and chill the beverages; keep an extra bag or two of ice in the freezer for backup. Set up the bar and table with platters, utensils, plates, napkins, and decorations.

⤵**2 hours before the party:** Bring the ham to room temperature. Prepare both salsas. Make the shrimp dip. Prepare the fritter mixture. Prepare the peanut sauce.

⤵**1 hour before the party:** Heat the ham according to the instructions. Pan-fry the salmon cakes and fritters, keep warm. Bake or grill the chicken skewers. Cover and keep warm.

⤵**$^1/_2$ hour before the party:** Set out the caramelized onions, eggplant spread, toasts, pita crisps, crackers, salsas, peanut sauce, mustards, and bread. Bring the fruit tartlets to room temperature. Just before guests arrive, set out the ham, shrimp dip, and warm hors d'oeuvres.

Breakfast

Breakfast foods needn't be limited to the morning; they can be eaten anytime, day or night. I've included recipes for an assortment of breakfast treats—from traditional egg dishes to pancakes and waffles to innovative savory dishes—all of which typically use milk, cream, butter, or cheese. Try any of these dairy-free recipes as a quick bite, a leisurely brunch, hors d'oeuvres, or a gratifying supper. Whatever your pleasure, these breakfasts hold no boundaries and are positively delicious.

Smoothies

Cool and refreshing smoothies are a great way to start the day or as a quick pick-me-up after a workout. They are also a great alternative to milk-shakes because they satisfy the desire for something sweet, icy cold, and creamy. Health food stores carry a wide variety of nutritional powder sup-plements, which can be added to any smoothie. When purchasing one of these supplements, be sure to check the ingredi-ents label very carefully, as many contain dairy and dairy derivatives.

Basic Smoothie Recipe

A combination of two or three of your favorite fruits, fresh or frozen

Any combination of the following: juice, rice or soy milk, soft tofu, soy yogurt, or sorbet

Ice (optional; omit if using frozen fruit)

Combine all of the ingredients in a blender and whirl at top speed for approx-imately 1 minute, or until smooth. Pour into a glass, slide in a straw, and enjoy.

Blueberry Banana Smoothie

1 ripe banana, cut into 2-inch chunks
1 cup fresh blueberries

$3/4$ cup orange juice
$3/4$ cup rice milk or soy milk
$1/2$ cup ice cubes (optional)

Blend as instructed in the Basic Smoothie Recipe.

Tropical Inspiration

1 cup cubed pineapple
1 cup sliced fresh mango
1 ripe banana, cut into 2-inch chunks
6 ounces drained silken soft or soft tofu, drained

$1/2$ cup pineapple juice
1 cup vanilla rice milk or vanilla soy milk
$1/4$ teaspoon coconut extract (optional)
$1/2$ cup ice cubes (optional)

Blend as instructed in the Basic Smoothie Recipe.

Mocha Cappuccino Smoothie

$1/2$ cup vanilla rice milk or vanilla soy milk
6 ounces silken soft or soft tofu, drained

$3/4$ cup strong coffee, chilled
$2/3$ cup chocolate sorbet
$1/2$ cup ice cubes
2 tablespoons sugar

Blend as instructed in the Basic Smoothie Recipe.

Sourdough French Toast

4 large eggs

1¹/₂ cups vanilla rice milk or
    vanilla soy milk

16 slices day-old sourdough French
    bread, sliced ¹/₂ inch thick

2 tablespoons pareve margarine

......

Toppings

Pareve margarine

Pure maple syrup, warmed

Confectioners' sugar for dusting
    (optional)

🔃 **To prepare the egg and bread:** Whisk together the eggs and rice milk in a bowl until well blended. Pour the egg mixture into an 8 by 11 by 2-inch baking dish or a shallow bowl. Soak the bread in the egg mixture, turning to coat and saturate both sides, for 3 to 4 minutes.

🔃 **To grill the toast:** Preheat a griddle or heavy skillet over medium-high heat (375° for an electric griddle). Melt the margarine on the hot griddle. Place the egg-soaked bread onto the hot grill. Grill for about 3 minutes, or until lightly browned. Using a spatula, carefully turn over the bread and continue grilling for 3 to 4 minutes more, or until lightly browned on the other side. Serve immediately with margarine, warm maple syrup, and a dusting of confectioners' sugar.

The smell of sourdough French toast always gets my family out of bed in a hurry. The combination of sweet maple syrup with sourdough bread makes for a wonderful taste sensation. Any type of bread can be used here, but the absorbent sourdough retains the flavorful vanilla batter perfectly. Serve with margarine and pure maple syrup, or top with sliced fresh fruit and a dusting of confectioners' sugar.

Smoked Sausage and Green Onion Waffles

Topping these waffles with homemade applesauce (page 122) or eggs over easy are just some of the ways to enjoy them. Have them for supper, or freeze them for after-school snacks or for a savory breakfast on the run. Just thaw, heat, and serve.

$1^1/_2$ cups flour
$^1/_2$ cup finely ground yellow
cornmeal
1 tablespoon baking powder
1 tablespoon sugar
$^1/_4$ teaspoon salt
$1^1/_2$ cups precooked smoked
chicken sausage (about
$^1/_2$ pound), finely chopped
1 cup minced green onions, both
white and green parts (about
1 bunch)

1 teaspoon minced fresh flat-leaf
parsley
3 large eggs
$^1/_4$ cup pareve margarine, melted
and cooled
2 cups vanilla rice milk or vanilla
soy milk
3 cups Applesauce (page 122), or
1 (24-ounce) jar applesauce

Lightly grease and preheat a waffle iron.

↪ **To prepare the batter:** Combine the flour, cornmeal, baking powder, sugar, and salt in a large bowl and mix together with a whisk. Add the sausage, green onion, and parsley, toss to coat, and set aside. In a separate bowl, whisk together the eggs, margarine, and rice milk until well blended. Pour the egg mixture into the flour mixture and stir with a large spoon until just combined.

↪ **To make the waffles:** Preheat the oven to 200°. With a ladle, pour about $^2/_3$ cup of the prepared batter into the center of the preheated waffle iron and close the top. Cook until the waffle is golden brown and steam no longer escapes, 4 to 5 minutes. Remove the waffle from the iron and place on a wire rack in the oven. Continue making waffles until all of the batter has been used. Serve with applesauce.

↪ **To store the waffles,** transfer the hot waffles to cooling racks and allow them to cool completely. Store in plastic freezer bags or in an airtight container, separating each pair of waffles with a piece of plastic wrap. Freeze. Waffles will keep in the freezer for up to 2 weeks.

Strawberry Banana Pancakes

2 cups flour

2 teaspoons baking powder

$^1/_2$ teaspoon salt

2 large eggs

1 tablespoon pareve margarine,
    melted and cooled

$1^1/_2$ cups vanilla rice milk or
    vanilla soy milk

$^1/_2$ cup fresh strawberries, cut into
    $^1/_2$-inch pieces

1 small ripe banana, cut into
    $^1/_2$-inch pieces

Toppings

Pareve margarine

Pure maple syrup, warmed

......

To prepare the batter: Combine the flour, baking powder, and salt in a large bowl and mix together with a whisk. In a separate bowl, whisk together the eggs, margarine, and rice milk until blended. Pour the egg mixture into the flour mixture and whisk until the batter is smooth. With a spoon, lightly stir in the strawberries and the banana until just combined.

To make the pancakes: Preheat a griddle or heavy skillet over medium-high heat (375° on an electric griddle). Lightly grease the griddle with pareve margarine. Ladle enough batter onto the hot griddle to make a 6-inch-diameter pancake. Cook until bubbles form and cover the pancake's surface, 2 to 3 minutes, and then flip the pancake over, using a spatula. Continue to cook the pancake on the other side for 2 to 3 minutes, or until it is golden brown. Continue making pancakes until all of the batter has been used. Serve immediately with margarine and warm maple syrup.

Makes about eighteen 6-inch pancakes

However you like your pancakes—thick or thin—these are sure to please. My mom would make these by the dozen, as the five of us kids vied to see who could eat the most. (One of my brothers would always win.) Today, we still make these all-time favorites, but fortunately as adults, we've cut back on the number we eat. If you like your pancakes thicker, use a little less rice or soy milk. If thinner pancakes are your pleasure, use a little more.

German Apple Pancake

Serves 4

This baked pancake is surprisingly easy to make and look impressive when served at the table. Unlike traditional pancakes, where the cook stands guard over the griddle, this version does most of its cooking in the oven. Be sure to have your guests gathered at the table, because once the pancake is pulled from the oven, it quickly deflates. To turn the pancake into a delightful dessert reminiscent of warm apple pie à la mode, add 1 tablespoon of brandy to the batter, and top each serving with a scoop of soy vanilla ice cream.

Apples

1 pound Pippin or Granny Smith apples, peeled, cored and thinly sliced
3 tablespoons sugar
1/2 teaspoon ground cinnamon
2 tablespoons freshly squeezed lemon juice
5 tablespoons pareve margarine

Batter

3 large eggs
3/4 cup vanilla rice milk or vanilla soy milk
3/4 cup flour
1/4 teaspoon salt

Toppings

Confectioners' sugar
Pure maple syrup, warmed

To prepare the apples: Combine the apples, sugar, cinnamon, and lemon juice in a bowl and toss to coat the apples. Melt 2 tablespoons of the margarine in a large sauté pan over medium-high heat. Add the apple mixture and sauté the apples until just soft, 6 to 8 minutes. Meanwhile, preheat the oven to 450°. Place the remaining 3 tablespoons margarine in a baking dish measuring 8 by 11 by 2 inches, and place the dish in the oven until the margarine is melted. Distribute the apples evenly over the bottom of the dish.

To prepare the batter: Whisk together the eggs and rice milk in a bowl until well blended. Add the flour and salt and stir until just combined. The batter will be slightly lumpy. Slowly pour the batter over the apples. Bake until the pancake is golden brown and puffed, 20 to 22 minutes. Sprinkle with a dusting of confectioners' sugar. Cut into pieces and serve immediately with warm maple syrup.

Potato Pancakes

2 pounds russet potatoes

$^1/_4$ cup flour

1 teaspoon baking powder

1 teaspoon salt

$^1/_4$ teaspoon freshly ground black
pepper

2 large eggs, beaten

4 green onions, both white and
green parts, thinly sliced

$^1/_4$ cup vegetable oil, canola or
safflower, more if needed

3 cups Applesauce (page 122) or
1 (24-ounce) jar applesauce

To prepare the potatoes: Place a pot of water over high heat. Add the potatoes in their skins and boil for about 15 to 20 minutes. They should still be slightly firm and not cooked completely through. Drain and rinse the potatoes under cold running water until the potatoes are cool enough to handle. Peel the potatoes and then, using the largest holes on a grater, grate them onto a plate.

To prepare the batter: In a large bowl, whisk together the flour, baking powder, salt, and pepper. Add the eggs, onions, and potatoes, and stir to blend.

To make the pancakes: Heat 2 tablespoons of the oil in a heavy nonstick skillet over medium-high heat. Spoon the batter by $^1/_4$ cupfuls onto the hot skillet, flattening them out slightly with the back of the spoon. Fry until the underside is golden brown, 3 to 5 minutes. Flip the pancakes over and cook for an additional 3 to 4 minutes. Transfer the pancakes to a plate layered with paper towels. Add more oil to the pan as needed, 2 tablespoons at a time, and continue cooking the pancakes until the batter is gone. Serve hot with applesauce.

Golden brown and crisp on the outside, moist and tender on the inside, these delicious griddle cakes are surprisingly simple to make. Use high-quality oil to fry the pancakes, making sure it is very hot before you add the batter. This will ensure light, crispy pancakes every time. Have them for breakfast or alongside grilled pork chops for dinner, but definitely serve them with applesauce.

Eggs Florentine

This recipe offers a colorful and lighter spin on the original French classic eggs Benedict by using spinach and tomatoes in place of Canadian bacon. If you are making this dish for a large group, you can poach the eggs ahead of time and keep them covered in the refrigerator in a shallow pan of cold water for up to 24 hours. When ready to use, reheat the eggs by carefully slipping them into boiling water for no longer than 1 minute just before serving.

1 tablespoon white wine vinegar
8 large eggs
2^1/$_4$ pounds fresh spinach,
    stemmed and coarsely chopped

8 slices ripe red tomato
8 rounds of bread or English
    muffins halves, lightly toasted
Hollandaise Sauce (page 112)

⚭**If you are making the eggs in advance:** Fill a large bowl with cold water and ice and set aside.

⚭**To prepare the eggs:** Fill a large, well-greased sauté pan with 2 inches of water and place it over medium-high heat. Bring the water to a slow simmer, until tiny bubbles form on the bottom of the pan. Add the vinegar to the water to help set the egg whites. Break the eggs directly into the water, taking special care not to disturb the yolks. Poach the eggs in two or more batches, so as not to overcrowd them. Adjust the heat if necessary to keep the water at a slow simmer, and cook the eggs, uncovered, for about 3 minutes. Using a large slotted spoon, transfer the eggs to a platter or, if making the eggs in advance, to the ice water to stop the cooking. Skim off any egg white residue from the pan and continue to poach the remaining eggs.

⚭**To prepare the spinach:** Place a large pot fitted with a steaming basket and water over medium-high heat and bring to a boil. Place the spinach in the basket, cover, and steam until just wilted, about 2 minutes. Remove the basket from the heat and allow the spinach to cool slightly.

⚭**To assemble the dish:** Place 2 rounds of bread or 2 English muffin halves on each plate, and top each with a slice of tomato. Distribute the spinach evenly on top of the tomatoes, and place the poached eggs on top. Spoon the warm hollandaise sauce over the eggs and serve immediately.

Crab and Artichoke Frittata

10 large eggs

$^1/_2$ cup rice milk or soy milk

$^3/_4$ teaspoon salt

$^1/_4$ teaspoon freshly ground black
   pepper

2 red bell peppers, roasted (page
   169) and chopped

1 cup stemmed, chopped fresh
   spinach, tightly packed (about
   $^1/_2$ bunch)

2 tablespoons coarsely chopped
   fresh basil

$^1/_3$ pound freshly cooked shelled
   crabmeat

2 tablespoons olive oil

1 red onion, finely chopped

1 cup coarsely chopped artichoke
   hearts

2 cloves garlic, minced

To prepare the frittata: Whisk the eggs, rice milk, salt, and pepper together in a large bowl until well blended. Add the bell pepper, spinach, and basil, and stir until incorporated. Gently stir in the crabmeat, and set aside.

Heat the olive oil in a large 12-inch ovenproof skillet over medium-high heat, and sauté the onion and artichoke hearts until lightly browned, about 5 minutes. Decrease the heat to medium-low and sauté the garlic for about 1 minute. Slowly pour the egg mixture into the skillet and cook until the frittata is set in the middle but still slightly liquid on the top, 8 to 10 minutes. Meanwhile, preheat the oven broiler and set the rack about 6 inches from the heat source.

Transfer the skillet to the oven and place it under the broiler. Broil the frittata until it is firm on top and golden brown, 5 to 6 minutes. The frittata will rise under the broiler but will deflate quickly once it is removed from the heat. Let the frittata stand at room temperature for 10 minutes before transferring it to a platter and cutting it into wedges.

The colors and flavors of this frittata are deliciously appealing, making it a Mother's Day brunch favorite at our house (see page 4). Frittata is incredibly versatile and easy to prepare; take one on your next picnic, or try serving it as a light supper with a salad of vine-ripened tomatoes and whole basil leaves drizzled with extra virgin olive oil, balsamic vinegar, and a turn or two of coarse salt and cracked pepper. Sliced into bite-size pieces and served at room temperature, frittata also makes an attractive yet simple appetizer.

Spanish "Tortilla"

Vacations are always special, but our trip to Spain was a fun-filled food extravaganza. While staying with our friends Jorge and Blanca, we were treated to one of Blanca's specialties, a marvelous Spanish tortilla. A Spanish tortilla is simply a potato omelet and has nothing in common with its Mexican counterpart. It can be served for brunch, dinner, or as hors d'oeuvres (tapas), hot or at room temperature.

¹/₄ cup olive oil
3 pounds russet potatoes, peeled and cut into ¹/₈-inch-thick rounds

1 large yellow onion, thinly sliced
5 large eggs
¹/₄ cup rice milk or soy milk
¹/₄ teaspoon salt

To prepare the tortilla: Heat 2 tablespoons of the olive oil in an 8- or 9-inch nonstick skillet over medium-low heat. Place one-third of the potato slices in a single layer in the skillet. Evenly distribute half of the onions on top of the potato slices, and repeat the layers, with one-third potato, the remaining onion, and the remaining potato. Slowly cook the potatoes until they begin to soften, 8 to 10 minutes.

Meanwhile, whisk the eggs, rice milk, and salt in a bowl until well blended. Decrease the heat to low, and pour the egg mixture over the potatoes. Cover and cook the mixture until the egg is slightly firm and the potatoes underneath turn golden brown, about 10 minutes. Uncover, place a large plate upside down on top of the skillet, and flip the tortilla onto the plate by inverting the skillet. Return the skillet to medium-low heat, add the remaining 2 tablespoons oil, and slide the tortilla back into the skillet. Cook on the other side until golden brown, about 8 minutes. Transfer the tortilla to a platter and allow it to stand at room temperature for 5 minutes before slicing into wedges.

Hors d'Oeuvres and Starters

These versatile appetizers can quell a hungry appetite while

dinner is cooking or provide an elegant starter to a meal.

When going out to dinner with friends, we often suggest

that everyone gather at our home first for a glass of wine

and a few appetizers. Not only does this afford us time to

chat, it also brings a personal touch to the evening. The

appetizers in this chapter combine well for a cocktail party,

and many can be prepared in advance, allowing everyone

the opportunity to relax and enjoy the gathering.

Caramelized Balsamic Onions
with Mushrooms

Caramelizing the onions
and mushrooms allows
their flavors to mingle and
is well worth the time
involved. This dish is best
made 1 or 2 days ahead of
serving, as it improves
with age. Cover and store
it in the refrigerator for up
to 1 week, and simply
warm before using. You
can serve it as a spread or,
for a robust vegetable
dish, toss with tender
cooked green beans. It
also makes a flavorful
topping for a Spanish
"Tortilla" (page 20).

2 tablespoons olive oil

2 tablespoons pareve margarine

2 large yellow onions, very thinly
    sliced

2 medium red onions, very thinly
    sliced

$^1/_4$ pound fresh button mushrooms,
    thinly sliced

5 sprigs thyme

$^1/_2$ teaspoon sugar

$^1/_2$ teaspoon salt

$^1/_8$ teaspoon freshly ground black
    pepper

3 tablespoons balsamic vinegar

2 cloves garlic, minced

Toasted baguette slices, Garlic Pita
    Crisps (page 173), or crackers
    as accompaniment

To prepare the spread: Heat the olive oil and margarine in a large skillet over medium-low heat until the margarine is melted. Add the onions, mushrooms, thyme, sugar, salt, and pepper. Stir to coat. Cover and cook the mixture, stirring occasionally, for about 20 minutes. Remove the lid and add the vinegar and garlic. Stir to blend. Continue to cook the mixture, uncovered, until most of the liquid has evaporated and the onions have caramelized, 45 to 55 minutes. Remove the thyme sprigs, taste, and correct the seasoning.

To serve the spread: Allow the spread to reach room temperature, or warm it by placing it in a small saucepan and gently warming it over low heat, stirring occasionally, about 5 minutes. Serve it alongside toasted baguette slices, Garlic Pita Crisps, (page 173), or crackers.

Shrimp Dip with Belgian Endive and Petite Potatoes

Makes 1¹/₂ cups

8 petite red new potatoes
¹/₃ pound cleaned, cooked shrimp
    meat
¹/₃ cup pareve mayonnaise
1¹/₂ teaspoons freshly squeezed
    lemon juice
¹/₄ cup minced celery (about
    1 stalk)
¹/₄ cup red bell pepper, seeded,
    deribbed, and minced (about
    ¹/₂ pepper)

2 tablespoons chopped fresh chives
    (about 1 bunch)
¹/₄ teaspoon salt
¹/₈ teaspoon freshly ground black
    pepper
4 heads red Belgian endive,
    separated into spears
4 heads white Belgian endive,
    separated into spears

An attractive presentation and two distinct tastes in one make this appetizer perfect for a party of any size. The creamy shrimp combined with the slightly bitter crisp endive is one way to enjoy this dip, or place a little atop a petite young potato.

To prepare the potatoes: Place in a large pot fitted with a steaming basket and water over medium-high heat and bring to a boil. Place the whole potatoes in the steaming basket and cover with a tight-fitting lid. Steam until just tender, 10 to 12 minutes. Do not overcook. Immerse the steamed potatoes in cold water to stop the cooking process and drain. Refrigerate the whole potatoes until ready to use; they can be made 1 day ahead. Halve the potatoes just before serving.

To prepare the dip: Place the shrimp on a plate lined with paper towels. Place additional paper towels on top, and lightly press out any excess moisture. Combine the mayonnaise, lemon juice, celery, bell pepper, chives, salt, and pepper in a nonmetallic bowl, and stir to blend. Gently fold in the shrimp meat until incorporated. Cover with a tight-fitting lid and refrigerate. This dip can be made several hours ahead of serving.

To arrange the platter: Transfer the dip to a small bowl with a serving spoon, and place the bowl off to the side on a platter. Arrange the potato halves in a half circle around the dip. Next, alternate the endive spears in a half circle around the potatoes, forming a fanned sunburst of red and green.

Mediterranean Ratatouille

My Tete (Aunt) Danie's ratatouille is at the top of our family's list of adored foods. She used to prepare it from the summer bounty of vine-ripened tomatoes and vegetables from my uncle's garden and then can it, so that we could enjoy the taste of summer during the winter months. I remember it fondly, as it always graced her holiday table as part of the antipasto platter.

3 tablespoons olive oil
2 red onions, coarsely chopped
2 pounds Japanese or globe eggplant, unpeeled, cut into 1-inch pieces
1 large red bell pepper, seeded, deribbed, and cut into 1-inch pieces
1 large yellow bell pepper, seeded, deribbed and cut into 1-inch pieces
4 cloves garlic, minced
1 pound zucchini, halved lengthwise, and cut into 1-inch pieces

2 pounds ripe tomatoes, seeded and coarsely chopped (about 3 cups)
2 teaspoons coriander seeds
3 sprigs thyme
1 teaspoon minced fresh rosemary
1 bay leaf
1/2 teaspoon salt
1/4 teaspoon freshly ground black pepper
1/4 cup minced fresh flat-leaf parsley
1 tablespoon freshly squeezed lemon juice

To prepare the ratatouille: Heat the olive oil in a large sauté pan over medium-high heat, and sauté the onion until tender, about 3 minutes. Add the eggplant, peppers, and garlic, and sauté until tender, 8 to 10 minutes, stirring occasionally. Add the zucchini, tomato, coriander, thyme, rosemary, bay leaf, salt, and pepper, and sauté until blended, 2 to 3 minutes. Cover, decrease the heat to medium-low, and simmer until the vegetables are tender, stirring occasionally, about 20 minutes. Remove from the heat, add the parsley and lemon, and toss to incorporate. Remove the bay leaf and thyme sprigs, taste, and correct the seasonings. Transfer the ratatouille to a bowl and allow to cool. Cover and refrigerate. Serve cold, warm, or hot. It can be made 2 days ahead.

Eggplant Sesame Basil Spread

2 pounds Japanese or globe
    eggplant, peeled and sliced
    1 inch thick

Salt for salting eggplant

1/3 cup olive oil, plus more for
    brushing eggplant

1 cup chopped green onion, both
    white and green parts (about
    1 bunch)

3 cloves garlic, minced

1/4 cup chopped fresh basil

1 large, ripe tomato, peeled and
    quartered, with juices
    (page 166)

1 tablespoon freshly squeezed
    lemon juice

1 teaspoon sugar

1/2 teaspoon salt

1/4 teaspoon freshly ground black
    pepper

2 teaspoons sesame oil

1 tablespoon sesame seeds, toasted
    (page 175)

Herb Toasts (page 173), Garlic
    Pita Crisps (page 173), or
    crackers as accompaniment

Although the eggplant can be broiled, grilling it on the barbecue imparts a wonderful smoky flavor that pairs nicely with the nutty flavor of the toasted sesame seeds. Make this spread a day or two before you are planning to serve it to allow the flavors to fully merge. Serve with toasted baguette slices, pita crisps, or crackers.

To prepare the eggplant: With a knife, score the eggplant slices diagonally 5 or 6 times about 1/2 inch deep, and sprinkle both sides with salt. Line a colander with paper towels and place the eggplant in the colander to drain for about 45 minutes.

Preheat the oven broiler and set the rack about 6 inches from the heat source. Generously brush the eggplant with olive oil. Place the eggplant on a broiler pan, cut side up, and broil for 8 to 10 minutes. With tongs, turn the eggplant over and continue broiling for 8 to 10 minutes until it is very soft. Remove it from the oven and transfer it to a plate to cool for about 15 minutes.

Meanwhile, heat 1 tablespoon of the olive oil in a small skillet over medium-high heat. Sauté the green onion, garlic, and basil until the onion is softened, about 1 minute. Remove from the heat and set aside.

When the eggplant is cool enough to handle, cut it into 2-inch pieces. Place the eggplant, tomato, remaining olive oil (about 1/4 cup), lemon juice, sugar, salt, and pepper in a blender. Pulse about 10 times. The mixture should be slightly chunky. Stir in the onion mixture and the sesame oil, taste, and correct the seasonings. To serve, stir in half of the sesame seeds, and sprinkle the rest on top.

Salmon Cakes with Kiwi Papaya Salsa

The infusion of texture, delicate flavors, and brilliant colors make these salmon cakes irresistible. Serve them as a refreshing starter dish or, to serve them as an appetizer, simply make each cake a bit smaller. Serve topped with Kiwi Papaya Salsa (page 121).

Poaching Liquid

2 cups water

1 cup dry white wine

1 bay leaf

5 whole black peppercorns

4 sprigs parsley

^{1}/$_4$ cup chopped celery leaves
  (from about 2 stalks)

......

Salmon Cakes

1^1/$_2$ pounds salmon steaks or fillets

^{1}/$_2$ cup drained soft tofu
  (4 ounces)

1 large egg

^{1}/$_2$ cup pareve mayonnaise

^{1}/$_2$ teaspoon Dijon mustard

1 medium yellow onion, finely
  chopped

3 tablespoons olive oil, more if
  needed

1 red bell pepper, seeded, deribbed,
  and finely chopped

^{1}/$_2$ cup finely chopped celery

^{1}/$_4$ cup minced fresh flat-leaf
  parsley

2 cups bread crumbs (page 174)

To poach the salmon: Combine the water, wine, bay leaf, peppercorns, parsley, and celery leaves in a large sauté pan over medium-high heat. Bring the contents to a boil, and add the salmon. Decrease the heat to low, cover, and simmer for 6 to 8 minutes. Transfer the salmon to a plate and set aside to cool.

To make the salmon cakes: Beat the tofu, egg, mayonnaise, and mustard with an electric mixer in a bowl until creamy, about 2 minutes. Set aside.

In a sauté pan over medium-high heat, sauté the onion in 1 tablespoon of the olive oil until softened, about 3 minutes; transfer it to a large bowl. To the onion add the bell pepper, celery, and parsley. Flake the salmon into the onion mixture, discarding any bones and skin. Gently fold in the tofu mixture and ^{1}/$_4$ cup of the bread crumbs until just combined.

To assemble and panfry the salmon cakes: Place the remaining 1^3/$_4$ cups bread crumbs on a plate. Using your hands, form the salmon mixture into 18 patties. Place the patties in the bread crumbs and coat them on both sides. Heat the remaining 2 tablespoons olive oil over medium heat. Cook the salmon cakes until golden brown, 2 to 3 minutes per side. Serve immediately.

Asian Chicken Skewers with Spicy Peanut Sauce

Serves 6

Marinade

1 cup unsweetened coconut milk,
    well blended

$^1/_3$ cup freshly squeezed lime juice
    (3 to 4 limes)

3 tablespoons seasoned rice vinegar

1 tablespoon ground turmeric

1 tablespoon yellow curry powder

1 tablespoon hot pepper sauce

1 teaspoon sugar

1 teaspoon salt

......

4 skinless, boneless chicken breast
    halves

20 (6-inch) bamboo skewers,
    soaked in water for 1 hour

Spicy Peanut Sauce (page 116)

To prepare the marinade: Whisk together the coconut milk, lime juice, vinegar, turmeric, curry powder, hot pepper sauce, sugar, and salt in a small bowl until well blended. Set aside.

To marinate and bake the chicken: Cut each chicken breast half lengthwise into about 5 thin strips. Thread each strip of chicken completely onto a skewer, leaving about $^3/_4$ inch of the skewer exposed at one end. Place the skewers in a shallow baking dish or in a heavy self-sealing plastic bag. Pour the marinade over the skewers, covering them completely. Cover and marinate in the refrigerator, turning the skewers occasionally, for about 3 hours or overnight.

Preheat the oven to 425°. Remove the chicken skewers from the marinade, and arrange them on a large, rimmed nonstick baking sheet in a single layer. Discard the marinade. Bake the chicken until just cooked through, about 10 minutes. Transfer the skewers to a platter and serve alongside the peanut sauce.

A delectable, easy-to-handle little bite, perfect for entertaining. These Thai-style skewers make a great appetizer. Be sure to have plenty on hand, as they tend to disappear quickly. If you're planning to grill the chicken, wrap the ends of the skewers with a small piece of aluminum foil. In spite of soaking, the skewers will still burn on the grill. Grilling may entail a little more work, but it imparts a wonderful flavor, making it well worth the effort.

Swiss Chard and Almond Torta

Similar to frittata, these
savory bite-size hors
d'oeuvres are filled with
varied flavors and textures.
The combination of chard
with fresh herbs adds a
healthful flavor to the
eggs, while the toasted
almonds provide an unex-
pected finish. Either green
or red Swiss chard can be
used in this recipe; how-
ever, I love the look of the
brilliant ruby-red chard
alongside the deep green
leaves of the basil and
parsley.

3 tablespoons pareve margarine
$1/3$ cup bread crumbs (page 174)
2 tablespoons flour
$1/2$ teaspoon baking powder
$1/2$ teaspoon baking soda
$1/4$ teaspoon freshly ground black
*   pepper*
$1/4$ cup finely chopped almonds,
*   toasted (page 175)*
2 cups finely chopped red onion
*   (about 1 medium onion)*

2 cloves garlic, minced
$1^{3}/4$ cups finely chopped Swiss
*   chard leaves (4 to 5 stalks)*
$1/4$ cup chopped fresh basil
2 tablespoons chopped fresh
*   flat-leaf parsley*
1 tablespoon chopped fresh dill
4 large eggs
2 teaspoons freshly squeezed lemon
*   juice*

Preheat the oven to 300°. Melt 1 tablespoon of the margarine in an 8 by 8 by
2-inch baking dish by placing the dish in the oven. Remove from the oven and
swirl the margarine in the dish to coat the bottom and sides. Set aside.

To prepare the mixture: Combine the bread crumbs, flour, baking powder,
baking soda, and pepper in a large bowl. Mix with a whisk until blended. Add
the almonds and stir to blend.

Melt the remaining 2 tablespoons margarine in a large sauté pan over
medium-high heat. Add the onion and sauté until it is soft but not brown,
about 3 minutes. Add the garlic and Swiss chard, and sauté until the chard is
just wilted, 2 to 3 minutes. Remove from the heat and add the basil, parsley,
and dill. Add the greens and their liquid to the almond mixture, and toss to
coat. In a small bowl, whisk the eggs and lemon juice together until blended.
Stir the egg mixture into the greens until well incorporated. Pour the mixture
into the prepared dish and bake until the center is just set, 40 to 45 minutes.
Transfer the dish to a wire rack and let cool for about 20 minutes. Slice into
1-inch or $1^{1}/2$-inch bite-size squares.

Olive Anchovy Tapenade

Makes 2 cups

2 tablespoons olive oil
1 medium yellow onion, finely
  chopped
2 cloves garlic, minced
1/2 cup pitted minced kalamata
  olives or other brine-cured
  black olives
1/2 cup pitted minced green olives
4 canned anchovy fillets, minced
2 tablespoons finely chopped
  pimiento

1 tablespoon freshly squeezed
  lemon juice
1/4 teaspoon freshly ground black
  pepper
1/4 cup minced fresh basil leaves
2 tablespoons capers, drained
Toasted baguette slices, Garlic Pita
  Crisps (page 173), or crackers
  as accompaniment

To prepare the tapenade: Heat 1 tablespoon of the olive oil in a skillet over medium-high heat, and sauté the onion until tender, about 3 minutes. Add the garlic and sauté for about 30 seconds. Remove from the heat and allow the mixture to cool slightly.

Combine the olives, anchovies, pimiento, lemon juice, pepper, and cooled onion mixture in a container with a tight-fitting lid, using a rubber spatula to blend the mixture thoroughly. Gently stir in the basil and capers until just incorporated. Cover and refrigerate.

To serve the spread: Remove the tapenade from the refrigerator and allow it to reach room temperature. Serve the tapenade with toasted baguette slices, Garlic Pita Crisps (page 173), or crackers.

This tapenade has become a staple in our home. In addition to using it as a spread on crackers and sliced baguette, we've been known to add a spoonful to pasta sauce and salad dressings and to use it on sandwiches in place of mayonnaise. It's easy to make and will keep for up to 2 weeks when tightly covered in the refrigerator. If you're not fond of anchovies and choose to omit them, you'll still have a wonderful tapenade.

Southwestern Fritters

These scrumptious, colorful little fritters make a zesty first course served alongside a pile of greens tossed in vinaigrette, or a terrific party appetizer. The heat from the chiles can vary, so try a tiny taste before adding them to the mixture, and feel free to add more or less chile according to your liking. If you want to increase the heat, add a little more cayenne pepper to the recipe.

2 large eggs
$^1/_2$ cup finely chopped red onion (about $^1/_2$ small onion)
$^1/_2$ cup finely chopped red bell pepper (about $^1/_2$ pepper)
$^1/_2$ cup finely chopped green bell pepper (about $^1/_2$ pepper)
$^1/_2$ cup white corn kernels, fresh (about 1 ear) or frozen
2 tablespoons chopped fresh cilantro
2 jalapeño chiles, seeded and minced (See Note)

2 teaspoons chopped fresh marjoram
$^1/_2$ teaspoon finely grated lime or lemon zest
$^1/_2$ teaspoon salt
$^1/_8$ teaspoon cayenne pepper
7 tablespoons bread crumbs (page 174)
Corn oil for frying
Pico de Gallo (page 121)

To make the batter: Whisk the eggs in a large bowl to blend. Add the onion, bell peppers, corn, cilantro, jalapeño, marjoram, zest, salt, cayenne, and bread crumbs and mix until well blended. Set the mixture aside for about 15 minutes to allow the flavors to develop.

To panfry the fritters: Heat 3 tablespoons oil in a large nonstick skillet over medium-high heat. Using a soup spoon, scoop up approximately 1 tablespoon of the mixture. With the palm of your hand, compact and shape the mixture in the spoon. Gently slide the shaped spoonfuls, about 2 inches in diameter, into the hot oil. Fry until the underside is golden brown, about 3 minutes. Gently flip the fritters over and cook for 3 to 4 minutes more. Transfer the fritters to a plate lined with paper towels to drain. Add more oil to the pan as needed, 2 tablespoons at a time, and continue cooking the fritters until all of the batter has been used. Serve topped with the salsa.

Note: Use care when handling chile peppers, especially jalapeños and habaneros. Wear gloves to prevent your hands from burning and from transferring the capsaicin (the burning compound) to sensitive organs, such as eyes.

Curry Vegetable Wonton in Pepper Bean Sauce

Serves 6

Filling

1 tablespoon olive oil

1/2 cup minced green onion, both white and green parts, reserving 2 inches of the green tips (about 1 bunch)

2 cups grated zucchini (2 to 3 zucchini)

1 large red bell pepper, roasted (page 169) and minced

1 clove garlic, minced

1/2 teaspoon yellow curry powder

1/4 teaspoon salt

1/4 teaspoon freshly ground black pepper

......

1 (12-ounce) package wonton skins

3 tablespoons canola oil for frying

2 cups Pepper Bean Sauce (page 113)

To prepare the filling: Place the olive oil in a large skillet over medium-high heat, and sauté the green onion until softened, about 2 minutes. Add the zucchini, bell pepper, garlic, curry powder, salt, and pepper. Sauté until the liquid has evaporated, 5 to 6 minutes. Taste and correct the seasonings.

To assemble the wontons: Lay 6 wonton skins out on a flat surface. Working quickly to prevent the skins from drying out, place about 1 tablespoon of the filling in the center of each wonton. Using a pastry brush, moisten the edges of the wonton skins with water. Fold the wonton wrapper in half, matching up the corners to form a triangle. Pinch the edges together to seal. Set each wonton with pinched edges pointing upward and the filled pouch as the base. Continue filling the remaining wonton skins.

To fry the wontons: Place the canola oil in a large skillet over high heat. Add the wontons 6 at a time to the hot skillet and fry until golden brown all over, about 3 minutes. Transfer the wontons to a plate lined with paper towels to drain.

To prepare the garnish: Cut the reserved green onion tips in half lengthwise. Open them so that they are flat on the cutting surface, and slice them lengthwise into very thin strips.

To serve, ladle some of the bean sauce in the center of each plate, and arrange 4 wontons in the center of the sauce. Scatter the green onion strips on top, and serve immediately.

This colorful, aromatic starter is a flavorful way to begin the evening. If you enjoy curries with heat, try some of the red and green pastes found in Asian markets—the selection is amazing. This recipe can easily be doubled and served as a buffet appetizer alongside a bowl of the Pepper Bean Sauce for dipping.

Scallop Prosciutto Bundles

There's so much visual drama in these elegant little bundles that they can be served as a fabulous first course or even as a light meal. The width of the prosciutto will determine how many slices will be necessary to assemble this dish. Ideally, the prosciutto should wrap completely around the scallop. To make the final wrapping a little easier, select the longest chives available.

⅓ cup dry white wine
¼ cup freshly squeezed lemon juice (about 2 lemons)
2 green onions, both white and green parts, minced
8 whole black peppercorns
1 bay leaf
12 fresh jumbo scallops
1 bunch fresh chives
6 to 12 paper-thin slices prosciutto
Freshly squeezed lemon juice for sprinkling over scallops

1½ cups finely shredded green cabbage (about ½ small head)
Olive oil for sprinkling over cabbage
Balsamic vinegar for sprinkling over cabbage
Freshly ground black pepper for sprinkling over cabbage
4 fresh lemon wedges for garnish (optional)

To poach the scallops: Combine the wine, lemon juice, green onion, peppercorns, and bay leaf in a large sauté pan over medium-high heat. Bring the contents to a boil, add the scallops, and decrease the heat to medium-low. Cook the scallops for 3 to 4 minutes, turning once. They should be just heated through; be careful not to overcook them, since they will be cooked further. With a slotted spoon, transfer the scallops to a plate to cool.

To prepare the chives: Fill a bowl with ice water and set aside. Bring a pot of water to a boil over high heat. Immerse the chives in the boiling water for 6 seconds. Quickly transfer the chives to the ice bath for about 15 seconds to stop the cooking. Remove the chives from the water, and place on a paper towel to drain.

To wrap the scallops and assemble the bundles: Lay 1 slice of prosciutto on a flat work surface. If the slice is wide, cut it in half lengthwise into 1-inch wide strips. Place a scallop at the far end of the prosciutto and gently roll the scallop up in the prosciutto, leaving the sides of the scallop exposed. Lay a chive down on the work surface, and place the wrapped scallop in the center of the chive. Tie the chive around the bundle, as if wrapping a package, and tie a knot. Continue until all of the scallops have been wrapped.

Place a large nonstick skillet over medium-high heat. Place the bundles in the hot skillet and sprinkle with lemon juice. Cover, and sear the bundles until the scallops are heated through and the prosciutto begins to look transparent, about 4 minutes.

To serve, divide the cabbage equally among 4 individual plates, and sprinkle with olive oil, vinegar, and pepper. Arrange 3 bundles on each plate, and garnish with a lemon wedge. Serve warm.

Baked Oysters

Although my husband and I may disagree on the best way to savor oysters—raw with a dab of hot sauce or, as I prefer mine, baked—we enjoy them immensely. Living on the West Coast allows us to choose from a variety of fresh oysters, the most popular being the Pacific oyster. Pacific (Hood Canal, Samish Bay), Kumamoto, and European flat (also know as Belon) are all suitable for this dish.

Filling

1/4 cup pareve margarine

1/3 cup minced fennel bulb or
    celery (about 1 bulb)

1/4 cup minced yellow onion
    (about 1/2 small onion)

2 tablespoons chopped fresh
    flat-leaf parsley

2 cloves garlic, minced

2 cups finely chopped fresh
    spinach, tightly packed (about
    1 small bunch)

1/4 teaspoon hot pepper sauce, or
    to taste

1 tablespoon freshly squeezed
    lemon juice

1/4 cup bread crumbs (page 174)

1/4 cup chopped pine nuts

......

24 fresh shucked oysters with their
    shells

1 head radicchio

To prepare the filling: Melt the margarine in a large skillet over medium-high heat, and sauté the fennel, onion, parsley, and garlic until tender, about 5 minutes. Add the spinach and sauté until it begins to wilt, about 2 minutes. Remove the skillet from the heat and add the hot pepper sauce and lemon juice, stirring to blend. Add the bread crumbs and nuts, tossing until incorporated and the mixture is uniformly moist.

To assemble and bake the dish: Preheat the oven to 425°. Line a shallow baking pan with rock salt about 1/2 inch deep, to prevent the shells from rocking. Place the oysters in the bottom half shell, and position them in the salt. Spoon about 1 teaspoon of the filling on top of each oyster. Bake the oysters until the edges begin to curl, 10 to 12 minutes.

To serve, shred the radicchio and arrange it on 4 individual plates. Place 6 oysters, in their shells, on each plate, and serve warm.

Salads and Dressings

Salads and dressings have come a long way over the years, with more flavorful combinations of ingredients than ever. Now that markets are carrying a wide assortment of lettuces, oils, and vinegars, it's easy to invent your own unique combinations. The dressings in this chapter embody a light, creamy, and smooth texture and can be prepared in no time. When making dressing, a good rule of thumb is to mix 3 parts oil to 1 part vinegar. This is not a steadfast rule, and depending on your palate, you may prefer a more acidic or milder dressing. If you have the time, make a dressing 2 to 24 hours in advance to allow the flavors time to fully blend. Also, be sure to mix the dressing well and taste and correct the seasonings before you toss it with a salad.

Spinach, Pear, and Beet Salad with Sherry Dressing

This winter salad makes an ideal starter for a Christmas dinner. The tender, dark green spinach, earthy beets, slightly sweet pear, and crimson cranberries give this salad a complexity of textures, colors, and flavors. For salads, I prefer the flavor of baked beets to boiled. The baking process makes them incredibly sweet while still retaining their natural flavor.

3 medium red or golden beets, trimmed

......

Dressing

1 cup peeled, cored, and diced ripe Bartlett or Bosc pear (1 or 2 pears)

$^1/_4$ cup dry sherry

$^1/_4$ cup olive oil

2 tablespoons freshly squeezed lemon juice

1 small shallot, chopped

1 teaspoon Dijon mustard

$^1/_2$ teaspoon sugar

$^1/_4$ teaspoon salt

$^1/_8$ teaspoon freshly ground black pepper

......

Salad

6 cups stemmed baby spinach leaves, lightly packed (about 1 bunch)

3 ripe Bartlett or Bosc pears, peeled, cored, and cut into $^1/_4$-inch-thick slices

$^1/_3$ cup dried cranberries

To prepare the beets: Preheat the oven to 425°. Wrap the beets individually in aluminum foil, enclosing them completely. Place the beets in the oven and roast for about 1 hour and 15 minutes, or until tender when pierced with a fork. Allow the beets to cool completely, about 2 hours or overnight. Using a sharp paring knife, peel the beets and slice them $^1/_2$ inch thick.

To prepare the dressing: Combine the pear, sherry, olive oil, lemon juice, shallot, mustard, sugar, salt, and pepper in a blender, and purée until smooth. Taste and correct the seasonings.

To assemble the salad: Place the spinach in a large bowl. Pour the dressing over the greens and toss to coat. Divide the greens equally among 4 to 6 plates. Arrange the pear slices and beets atop the greens, and scatter the cranberries over them. Serve immediately.

Mixed Greens with Citrus and Candied Pecans

Serves 6

Dressing

$^1/_4$ cup pareve mayonnaise

2 tablespoons olive oil

2 tablespoons freshly squeezed
    lemon juice

2 tablespoons frozen orange juice
    concentrate, thawed

1 tablespoon seasoned rice vinegar

$^1/_2$ teaspoon balsamic vinegar

1 teaspoon honey

$^1/_4$ teaspoon salt

$^1/_4$ teaspoon freshly ground black
    pepper

......

Salad

2 ruby grapefruit

2 heads romaine hearts, torn into
    bite-size pieces

4 cups mixed greens (an assort-
    ment of frisée, radicchio,
    arugula, escarole, and
    watercress)

$^3/_4$ cup Candied Pecans
    (page 176)

I prepared this salad for 120 ladies at a spring luncheon, and it got rave reviews. It's light, colorful, and refreshing, with the tangy grapefruit providing a nice contrast to the sweet candied pecans. Many supermarkets now carry an assortment of mixed greens in bulk or prewashed in bags, making it convenient to add variety to your salads.

To prepare the dressing: Whisk together the mayonnaise, olive oil, lemon juice, orange juice concentrate, vinegars, honey, salt, and pepper in a small bowl until well blended. Taste and correct the seasonings. Cover and refrigerate for 1 hour or up to 5 days.

To prepare the grapefruit: Peel the grapefruits and remove all of the white pith. Working over a bowl, cut the grapefruit between the membranes to release the segments. Spoon 2 tablespoons of the dressing over the segments to coat. Let stand for 15 minutes or up to 1 hour.

To assemble the salad: Toss the greens together in a large bowl until well combined. Pour the remaining dressing over the greens, and toss to coat. Divide the greens equally among 6 plates. Arrange the grapefruit segments on top of the greens, and scatter the pecans on top. Serve immediately.

Sweet and Tangy Jicama Slaw

Crunchy jicama is a nice addition to this summertime classic, adding a unique texture and flavor not found in common coleslaw. Cool and crisp, it's a great complement to meats barbecued with the Southern Spicy Rub (page 125).

Dressing

1/3 cup pareve mayonnaise

2 tablespoons freshly squeezed lime juice

2 tablespoons seasoned rice vinegar

1 tablespoon sugar

1/4 teaspoon salt

1/8 teaspoon freshly ground black pepper

......

Salad

4 cups shredded green cabbage (about one 1-pound head)

2 cups peeled, julienned jicama, in 1 1/2-inch strips (about 1 small jicama)

2 carrots, peeled and cut into 1 1/2-inch julienne strips

1 red bell pepper, seeded, deribbed, and cut into 1 1/2-inch julienne strips

1/2 cup coarsely chopped green onion, both white and green parts (about 1/2 bunch)

1/3 cup chopped flat-leaf parsley (about 1/2 bunch)

To prepare the dressing: Whisk together the mayonnaise, lime juice, vinegar, sugar, salt, and pepper in a small bowl until well blended. Set aside.

To assemble the salad: Combine the cabbage, jicama, carrot, green onion, and parsley in a large bowl. Toss to mix. Pour the dressing over the salad and toss until well incorporated. Taste and correct the seasonings. Cover and refrigerate for 1 to 3 hours. Toss the salad again before serving.

Chicken Salad

4 boneless, skinless chicken breast
   halves, about 6 ounces each

Dressing

$3/4$ cup pareve mayonnaise

3 tablespoons apple cider vinegar

1 tablespoon honey

1 tablespoon poppyseeds

$1/2$ teaspoon salt

$1/4$ teaspoon ground white pepper

Salad

1 cup thinly sliced celery (about
   3 stalks)

$1/2$ cup thinly sliced green onion,
   both white and green parts
   (about $1/2$ bunch)

1 cup red seedless grapes

$1/2$ cup pecan halves, toasted
   (page 175)

2 tablespoons chopped fresh
   flat-leaf parsley

To prepare the chicken: Fill a stockpot with water and bring to a boil over high heat. Add the chicken to the boiling water, cover, and return to a boil. Boil the chicken for 2 to 3 minutes. Turn off the heat, and let the chicken steep, covered, until it is no longer pink in the thickest part of the breast, 10 to 15 minutes. Using a slotted spoon, transfer the chicken to a plate and let cool for approximately 20 minutes. Meanwhile, prepare the dressing.

To prepare the dressing and assemble the salad: Whisk together the mayonnaise, vinegar, honey, poppyseeds, salt, and pepper in a large bowl until well blended. Cut the cooked, cooled breast meat into $3/4$-inch cubes; you should have about 4 cups. Add the chicken, celery, onion, grapes, pecans, and parsley to the dressing. Toss to coat. Taste and correct the seasonings. Serve immediately.

This salad is as delicious as it is pretty and makes a terrific luncheon main course. I like to serve it tumbling out of a split Orange Cornmeal Popover (page 133), resting on a bed of butter lettuce. Steeping the chicken breasts produces tender and succulent meat that is ideal for a salad. As an alternative, roast chicken with the skin and bones removed also works well. Figure on one 2-pound roast chicken, yielding about 4 cups of cubed or shredded meat.

Asian Peanut Pasta Salad

This Asian-influenced chilled noodle salad is a success at parties, pleasing adults and kids alike. It can be served as a starter but makes a fantastic main course as well. The addition of Pan-Seared Tofu (page 106) adds a substantial amount of protein as well as delicious flavor from its marinade.

1 (12-ounce) package chow mein noodles or spaghetti

1 tablespoon sesame oil

4 cups shredded napa cabbage (about one 1-pound head)

1 red bell pepper, seeded, deribbed, and cut into 1½-inch julienne strips

2 carrots, peeled and cut into 1½-inch julienne strips

2 tablespoons chopped fresh flat-leaf parsley

4 green onions, both white and green parts, thinly sliced

1 cup Spicy Peanut Sauce (page 116)

Pan-Seared Tofu (page 106), chilled and cut into ½-inch cubes

To cook the pasta: Bring 3 quarts of water to a boil in a large saucepan over high heat. Add the pasta to the water. Allow the water to return to a boil and stir. Cook the pasta, uncovered, according to the package directions, taking care not to overcook it. Drain the pasta in a colander, rinse under cold running water, and drain again. Transfer the pasta to a large bowl and toss with the sesame oil to coat.

To assemble the salad: Place the cabbage, bell pepper, carrot, parsley, and green onion in a large bowl. Pour the peanut sauce over the vegetables, and toss to coat. Add the pasta and tofu, and gently toss until well combined. Serve immediately, or cover and refrigerate for up to 1 day. If refrigerated, bring to room temperature before serving.

Black Bean and Corn Salad

Dressing

2 tablespoons seasoned rice wine
    vinegar

1 tablespoon olive oil

$^1/_2$ teaspoon freshly squeezed
    lemon juice

$^1/_4$ teaspoon salt

$^1/_8$ teaspoon freshly ground black
    pepper

......

Salad

$^1/_2$ cup finely chopped red onion
    (about $^1/_2$ small onion)

2 cups white corn kernels, fresh
    (4 to 6 ears) or frozen

4 cups cooked black beans (page
    170), rinsed well, or canned
    beans

1 red bell pepper, seeded, deribbed,
    and chopped into $^1/_4$-inch
    pieces

$^1/_3$ cup minced fresh cilantro

This colorful salad is perfect for summer gatherings. It is quick and easy to prepare, keeps well, and tastes great too. The combination of tender black beans, crunchy red peppers, refreshing cilantro, and sweet corn is a delight to the palate. I prefer using fresh white corn to yellow because I find it to be sweeter and more tender; however, yellow corn works equally well.

To prepare the dressing: Whisk together the vinegar, olive oil, lemon juice, salt, and pepper in a small bowl until blended. Set aside.

To prepare the onion: Immerse the chopped onion in a bowl of cold water and swish it occasionally to release some of its sharp, acidic flavor, about 10 minutes. Drain the water and refill the bowl with fresh water. Repeat the process until the onion has soaked for about 40 minutes. Drain the onion, and blot it dry with paper towels.

To prepare the corn: Bring 4 cups of water to a boil in a saucepan over high heat. Meanwhile, toss the corn kernels with your fingers to break up any that are stuck together. Place the kernels in a fine metal strainer, and immerse the corn in the boiling water until the corn is just tender, about 2 minutes. Remove the strainer and drain. Rinse the kernels with cold running water to stop the cooking, and drain again.

To assemble the salad: Place the beans, corn, onion, and bell pepper in a large bowl and toss to mix. Add the dressing to the bean mixture, and gently toss until just incorporated. Cover and refrigerate for about 2 hours. Add the cilantro and toss again before serving. Taste and correct the seasonings.

Creamy Tarragon Dressing

Makes 1 cup

This versatile dressing lends itself nicely to a wide variety of vegetables and salad greens as well as meat and fish dishes. For a taste of the French countryside, drizzle it over a bed of watercress, tomato, cucumber, and sliced chicken or fish, and enjoy a delicate luncheon salad.

$^1/_4$ cup white wine vinegar
$^1/_3$ cup extra virgin olive oil
3 tablespoons minced fresh
   tarragon
2 tablespoons minced fresh chives
1 clove garlic, minced

1 tablespoon Dijon mustard
2 tablespoons pareve mayonnaise
1 teaspoon sugar
$^1/_8$ teaspoon salt
$^1/_8$ teaspoon freshly ground black
   pepper

To prepare the dressing: Whisk together the vinegar, olive oil, tarragon, chives, garlic, mustard, mayonnaise, sugar, salt, and pepper in a bowl. Transfer the dressing to a container with a tight-fitting lid, cover, and refrigerate for at least 2 hours or overnight. Before serving, mix to blend, and taste and correct the seasonings. The dressing will keep for 5 days in the refrigerator, tightly covered.

Thousand Island Dressing

Makes 1 cup

For a simple salad, toss this dressing with romaine or iceberg lettuce and tomato, or serve it alongside a seafood salad of fresh shrimp or crab, hard-boiled eggs, and slices of tomato and avocado.

$^1/_2$ cup pareve mayonnaise
3 tablespoons ketchup
1 hard-boiled egg, minced
$1^1/_2$ tablespoons sweet pickle relish
1 tablespoon minced chives or
   green onion, green part only

$^1/_2$ teaspoon freshly squeezed
   lemon juice
$^1/_8$ teaspoon freshly ground black
   pepper

To prepare the dressing: Whisk together the mayonnaise, ketchup, egg, relish, chives, lemon juice, and pepper in a bowl. Transfer the dressing to a container with a tight-fitting lid. Cover and refrigerate for at least 2 hours or overnight. Before serving, mix to blend, and taste and correct the seasonings. The dressing will keep for 1 week in the refrigerator, tightly covered.

Creamy Avocado Dressing

Makes 1 cup

1 ripe avocado, halved, peel and
    pit removed
$^1/_3$ cup rice milk or soy milk
2 tablespoons freshly squeezed
    lemon juice
1 tablespoon extra virgin olive oil

2 tablespoons pareve mayonnaise
$^1/_2$ teaspoon fresh dill, or
    $^1/_4$ teaspoon dried
$^1/_4$ teaspoon salt
$^1/_8$ teaspoon ground white pepper

To prepare the dressing: Combine the avocado, rice milk, lemon juice, olive oil, mayonnaise, dill, salt, and pepper in a blender. Whirl at top speed until smooth, about 1 minute, scraping down the sides with a rubber spatula. Transfer the dressing to a container with a tight-fitting lid; cover and refrigerate for at least 2 hours or overnight. Before serving, mix to blend, and taste and correct the seasonings. This dressing will keep for 5 days in the refrigerator, tightly covered.

This dressing tastes sinfully rich and delicious, but avocados are actually low in fat and high in vitamins E, C, and B$_6$. Try serving this dressing with tacos or tostadas, or atop fresh vine-ripened tomatoes, sliced and arranged on a bed of butter lettuce.

Summer Fruit Salad Dressing

Makes 1$^1/_2$ cups

$^1/_4$ cup freshly squeezed lime juice
    (2 to 3 limes)
1 teaspoon minced lime zest

1 tablespoon minced fresh cilantro
1 tablespoon frozen orange juice
    concentrate, thawed

To prepare the dressing: Whisk together the lime juice, zest, cilantro, and orange juice concentrate in a small bowl until blended. This dressing is best served immediately.

This tangy dressing will make your next fruit salad sing. Try serving it with sliced nectarines, peaches, or plums, in combination with papaya, blueberries, and raspberries for a dazzling and delicious display.

Creamy Papaya Vinaigrette

This dressing is delightful in the summertime, when papayas are at their peak. It's light and fruity, evoking a taste of the tropics with every bite. The luscious fruit is perfectly balanced by the tart lime juice, and the vanilla rice milk makes it creamy. Drizzle it over fresh fruit, or toss it with tender greens, tangerine slices, and a handful of poppyseeds.

1 ripe papaya, peeled, seeded, and
   cut into quarters
¹/₄ cup vanilla rice milk or vanilla
   soy milk
3 tablespoons freshly squeezed lime
   juice (about 2 limes)

2 tablespoons pareve mayonnaise
2 tablespoons apple cider vinegar
¹/₄ teaspoon salt

To prepare the dressing: Place the papaya, rice milk, lime juice, mayonnaise, vinegar, and salt in a blender. Whirl at top speed until smooth, about 1 minute. Transfer the dressing to a container with a tight-fitting lid; cover and refrigerate for at least 2 hours or overnight. Before serving, whisk the dressing to blend, and taste and correct the seasonings. The dressing will keep for 5 days in the refrigerator, tightly covered.

Soups

Soups are a wonderful way to start a meal and are often hearty enough to be a main course. Once you have a few fundamental techniques established, whipping up a nurturing bowl of hot soup on a cold winter day becomes effortless. I often double a recipe and freeze the extra in small batches for future use. I line a measuring cup with a heavy, self-sealing plastic freezer bag, making it easy to ladle and store the exact amount for a meal. All of the soups in this chapter are simple to prepare, flavorful, and satisfying. Many are so luscious and creamy that, if you hadn't made them yourself, you would think they were made with heavy cream. Any of the soups that use chicken stock as the base can easily be transformed into vegan soups simply by preparing them with vegetable stock.

Carrot and Roasted Red Pepper Soup

Rich and vibrant in color with a lightly roasted flavor, this soup makes a wonderful first course. It can be prepared up to 2 days in advance. Allow the soup to cool, then refrigerate it in a tightly covered container. Rewarm the soup over low heat, stirring occasionally, until hot.

1 pound carrots, peeled and cut into 2-inch pieces
2 large red bell peppers, roasted (page 169) and cut into quarters
1 large yellow onion, coarsely chopped
2¹/₂ cups chicken stock (page 164)
³/₄ cup dry white wine
¹/₈ teaspoon ground cumin
¹/₂ teaspoon salt
¹/₈ teaspoon freshly ground black pepper
³/₄ cup rice milk or soy milk, more if needed
1 tablespoon minced roasted red bell pepper for garnish (optional)

To prepare the soup: In a saucepan, combine the carrots, roasted peppers, onion, chicken stock, white wine, cumin, salt, and pepper. Bring to a boil. Cover, decrease the heat, and simmer until the vegetables are tender when pierced with a fork, about 25 minutes.

To purée the soup: Remove the soup from the heat, and ladle half of it into a blender, along with ¹/₂ cup of the rice milk. Purée until smooth. Empty the blender into a large bowl and repeat with the remaining soup and ¹/₄ cup rice milk. Transfer the puréed soup back to the saucepan. Thin the soup if necessary by adding a little more rice milk, ¹/₄ cup at a time, until the desired consistency is achieved. Taste and correct the seasonings. Reheat over low heat, stirring occasionally, until hot, taking care not to boil the soup. Ladle into bowls, and garnish with a sprinkling of minced roasted pepper.

Creamy Broccoli Soup

1¹/₂ pounds broccoli, cut into
    small florets
1 large yellow onion, coarsely
    chopped
1¹/₄ pounds russet potatoes, peeled
    and cut into 2-inch pieces
3 cups chicken stock (page 164)
¹/₂ cup dry white wine
¹/₄ teaspoon freshly squeezed
    lemon juice

2 bay leaves
¹/₂ teaspoon salt
¹/₈ teaspoon freshly ground black
    pepper
³/₄ cup rice milk or soy milk, more
    if needed
Grated lemon zest for garnish
    (optional)

To prepare the soup: Combine the broccoli, onion, potatoes, chicken stock, wine, lemon juice, bay leaves, salt, and pepper in a large saucepan. Bring to a boil. Cover, decrease the heat to low, and simmer until the vegetables are tender when pierced with a fork, about 25 minutes.

To purée the soup: Remove the soup from the heat and discard the bay leaves. Ladle half of the soup into a blender along with ¹/₂ cup of the rice milk, cover, and purée until smooth. Empty the blender into a large bowl and repeat with the remaining soup and ¹/₄ cup rice milk. Transfer the puréed soup back to the saucepan. Thin the soup if necessary by adding a little more rice milk, ¹/₄ cup at a time, until the desired consistency is achieved. Taste and correct the seasonings. Reheat over low heat, stirring occasionally, until hot, taking care not to boil the soup. Ladle into bowls and garnish with Herb Toasts (page 173) and lemon zest.

This mild, creamy soup is enhanced with just a hint of lemon. It's the only way I can get my husband to eat and enjoy broccoli. Not only does this soup taste great, but broccoli is a calcium-rich vegetable, and this soup is loaded with it.

Salmon and White Corn Chowder

Delicately flavored with a
slight sweetness from the
corn, this chowder is rich
in texture and taste. When
served with country Italian
or French bread and a
simple salad, it's a meal
in itself. Poaching the
salmon with the skin on
releases just enough oil
to enrich the broth.

3 (8-ounce) bottles clam juice
$^1/_4$ cup dry white wine
1 (16-ounce) salmon fillet with
   skin
$^1/_4$ cup pareve margarine
3 medium leeks, white and pale
   green parts only, thinly sliced
$1^1/_4$ pounds white potatoes, peeled
   and cut into $^1/_2$-inch pieces

5 tablespoons flour
$2^1/_2$ cups rice milk or soy milk
1 cup white corn kernels, fresh
   (about 2 ears) or frozen
$^1/_2$ teaspoon salt
$^1/_4$ teaspoon freshly ground black
   pepper
2 tablespoons minced green onion,
   green part only

To prepare the salmon: Bring the clam juice and wine to a boil in a saucepan over medium-high heat. Decrease the heat to low and add the salmon. Cover and simmer until cooked through, 8 to 10 minutes. With a slotted spoon, transfer the salmon to a plate and allow to cool, reserving the clam juice for later use. With a fork, flake the salmon into small pieces, discarding the skin and bones. Set aside.

To assemble the soup: Melt 1 tablespoon of the margarine in a large saucepan over medium-high heat. Add the leeks and sauté until soft, about 4 minutes. Add the reserved clam juice and the potatoes, and bring to a boil. Decrease the heat to low, cover, and simmer until the potatoes are tender, about 10 minutes.

Meanwhile, in a small saucepan over low heat, melt the remaining 3 tablespoons margarine. Using a wire whisk, add the flour, a little at a time, until the roux is well blended and thickened, 1 to 2 minutes. Whisk in the rice milk, a little at a time, until blended, about 2 minutes.

Add the milk mixture to the potato mixture and bring to a simmer over low heat. Stir in the salmon, corn, salt, and pepper, and cook over low heat until heated through, taking care not to boil the soup. Taste and correct the seasonings. Ladle the soup into bowls and garnish with green onions.

Yukon Gold Potato-Leek Soup

3 tablespoons pareve margarine

4 medium leeks, white and pale
    green part only, sliced 1 inch
    thick

$2^1/_2$ cups chicken stock (page 164)

$1^1/_2$ pounds Yukon Gold potatoes,
    peeled and cut into 2-inch
    pieces

$^1/_2$ teaspoon salt

$^1/_8$ teaspoon ground white pepper

$1^1/_4$ cups rice milk or soy milk,
    more if needed

Chives cut into 2-inch-long pieces
    for garnish (optional)

Incredibly rich in flavor and luxurious to the palate, Yukon Gold potatoes lend themselves nicely to this comforting classic.

To prepare the soup: Melt the margarine in a large saucepan over medium-high heat. Add the leek and sauté until it is soft but not brown, about 3 minutes. Add the chicken stock, potatoes, salt, and pepper; bring to a boil. Cover, decrease the heat to low, and simmer until the vegetables are tender when pierced with a fork, about 20 minutes.

To purée the soup: Remove the soup from the heat and ladle half of it into a blender, along with $^3/_4$ cup of the rice milk. Cover and purée until smooth. Empty the blender into a large bowl and repeat with the remaining soup and $^1/_2$ cup rice milk. Transfer the puréed soup back to the saucepan. Thin the soup if necessary by adding a little more rice milk, $^1/_4$ cup at a time, until the desired consistency is achieved. Taste and correct the seasonings. Reheat over low heat, stirring occasionally, until hot, taking care not to boil the soup. Ladle the soup into bowls and garnish with the chives by tossing them on top like scattered matchsticks.

Butternut Squash and Pear Soup

Bright tasting with a lovely color, this soup is delicious served during the fall and winter months. The hard pear cider provides a slightly sweet background flavor. For a simple yet satisfying meal, serve it alongside a salad of tart greens and Green Onion–Rosemary Drop Biscuits (page 135).

3 tablespoons pareve margarine

2$^{1}/_{2}$ pounds butternut squash, peeled, seeded, and cut into $^{1}/_{2}$-inch pieces (about 6 cups)

1 medium onion, coarsely chopped

2 cups chicken stock (page 164)

2 Bosc pears, peeled, cored, and cut into 2-inch pieces

1 (12-ounce) bottle hard pear cider

1 teaspoon freshly squeezed lemon juice

$^{1}/_{2}$ teaspoon salt

1 cup rice milk or soy milk, more if needed

Minced fresh parsley for garnish (optional)

To prepare the soup: Melt the margarine in a large saucepan over medium-high heat, and sauté the butternut squash and onion until softened but not brown, about 10 minutes. Add the chicken stock, pears, cider, lemon juice, and salt. Bring to a boil. Cover and decrease the heat to low. Simmer until the vegetables are tender when pierced with a fork, about 25 minutes.

To purée the soup: Remove the soup from the heat and ladle half of it into a blender along with $^{1}/_{2}$ cup of the rice milk. Cover and purée until smooth. Empty the blender and repeat with the remaining soup and $^{1}/_{2}$ cup rice milk. Transfer the puréed soup back to the saucepan. Thin the soup if necessary by adding a little more rice milk, $^{1}/_{4}$ cup at a time, until the desired consistency is achieved. Taste and correct the seasonings. Reheat over low heat, stirring occasionally, until hot, taking care not to boil the soup. Ladle into bowls and garnish with minced parsley.

White Bean Vegetable Soup

2 tablespoons olive oil

1 large yellow onion, coarsely
    chopped

3 cloves garlic, minced

1/2 small butternut squash, peeled,
    seeded, and cut into 1/2-inch
    pieces

3 carrots, peeled, sliced lengthwise,
    and cut into 1/2-inch pieces

2 stalks celery, cut into 1/4-inch
    dice

1 bunch kale, stemmed and finely
    chopped

5 cups chicken stock (page 164)

1 1/2 cups chopped tomatoes
    (page 166)

2 large sage leaves, chopped, or
    1/4 teaspoon dried sage,
    crumbled

1 tablespoon minced fresh parsley

1/2 teaspoon salt

1/8 teaspoon freshly ground black
    pepper

2 cups cooked white beans
    (page 170)

This Tuscan-style soup, with its healthful combination of calcium-rich vegetables and beans, takes the chill off cold winter days. I prefer using small white navy beans, but cannellini and lima beans are also delicious. Enjoy it with a warm slice of Sweet Potato Corn Bread (page 136).

To prepare the soup: Heat the olive oil in a large saucepan over medium-high heat and sauté the onion until tender, about 3 minutes. Add the garlic and cook another 30 seconds without letting it brown. Add the squash, carrot, celery, kale, chicken stock, tomato, sage, parsley, salt, and pepper. Bring to a boil. Cover and decrease the heat to low. Simmer the vegetables until the kale is tender, about 20 minutes. Add the beans and continue cooking for 10 to 15 minutes, stirring occasionally, to allow the flavors to fully develop. Ladle the soup into bowls and serve.

Three Mushroom Bisque

The rich aromas of this bisque will fill your senses with the earth and woods after a rain. Adding a pinch of cardamom in combination with the nutmeg is an effective way to draw out the soup's essence. Its deep, full-bodied flavor and color are further intensified by the fusion of fresh and dried mushrooms.

1/2 ounce dried porcini mushrooms
3/4 cup hot water
1 pound fresh button mushrooms, sliced
1 pound fresh portobello mushrooms, trimmed, and sliced into 1 1/2-inch strips (about 2 caps)
1 cup dry white wine
1 large yellow onion, coarsely chopped
4 cups chicken stock (page 164)

2 medium russet potatoes, peeled and cut into 2-inch pieces
1/4 cup chopped fresh flat-leaf parsley
1/2 teaspoon salt
1/4 teaspoon freshly ground black pepper
1/4 teaspoon ground nutmeg
Pinch ground cardamom
1 cup rice milk or soy milk, more if needed
Parsley sprigs for garnish (optional)

To reconstitute the mushrooms: Place the porcini mushrooms in a small bowl with the hot water. Allow them to soak for 20 minutes, swishing occasionally to loosen any grit. Lift the mushrooms out of the water with a slotted spoon. Using a fine sieve, strain the liquid over a small bowl to remove any sediment. Reserve the liquid and set aside.

To make the soup: In a large saucepan over medium-high heat, combine the porcini, button, and portobello mushrooms with 1/2 cup of the wine. Sauté, stirring frequently until all of the liquid has evaporated and the mushrooms are lightly browned, 12 to 15 minutes. Set aside 1/2 cup of the mushrooms for later use. To the remaining mushrooms, add the onion and the remaining 1/2 cup wine. Continue sautéing until the liquid is fully absorbed and the onions are softened, 3 to 5 minutes.

Add the stock, reserved mushroom liquid, potatoes, parsley, salt, pepper, nutmeg, and cardamom to the onion mixture. Bring to a boil. Cover, decrease the heat to low, and simmer until the potatoes are tender when pierced with a fork, about 25 minutes.

To purée the soup: Remove the soup from the heat, and ladle half of it into a blender, along with $^1/_2$ cup of the rice milk. Cover and purée until smooth, about 1 minute. Empty the blender and repeat with the remaining soup and $^1/_2$ cup rice milk. Transfer the puréed soup back to the saucepan, add the reserved mushrooms, and stir. Thin the soup if necessary by adding a little more rice milk, $^1/_4$ cup at a time, until the desired consistency is achieved. Taste and correct the seasonings. Reheat over low heat, stirring occasionally, until hot, taking care not to boil the soup. Ladle the soup into bowls and garnish with parsley sprigs.

Cabbage Bisque

This delicious, nourishing soup has a delightful, silky smooth texture. By first blanching the cabbage, you remove any potential bitterness. For an excellent addition to the Autumn Vegan Supper (page 6), simply substitute vegetable stock for the chicken stock.

$1^{1}/_{2}$ pounds green cabbage, halved and cored

2 tablespoons pareve margarine

1 large yellow onion, coarsely chopped

2 cups chicken stock (page 164)

$^{1}/_{3}$ cup dry white wine

$1^{1}/_{2}$ pounds russet potatoes, peeled and coarsely chopped

1 teaspoon minced fresh dill, or $^{1}/_{4}$ teaspoon dried

$^{1}/_{4}$ cup chopped fresh parsley

$^{3}/_{4}$ teaspoon salt

$^{1}/_{8}$ teaspoon ground white pepper

2 cups rice milk or soy milk, more if needed

To prepare the cabbage: Set it in a large bowl and pour enough boiling water over it to cover it completely. Let the cabbage stand until it has softened, about 8 minutes. Transfer the cabbage to a colander and drain well, about 20 minutes. Slice the drained cabbage into julienne strips about 2 inches long. Reserve 2 cups of the julienned cabbage in a small bowl, and set aside.

To make the soup: Melt the margarine in a large saucepan over medium-high heat. Add the onion and sauté until soft, about 3 minutes. Add the cabbage, chicken stock, wine, potatoes, dill, parsley, salt, and pepper. Bring to a boil, cover, decrease the heat to low, and simmer until the vegetables are tender, about 25 minutes.

To purée the soup: Remove the soup from the heat and ladle half of it into a blender, along with 1 cup of the rice milk. Cover and purée until smooth, about 1 minute. Empty the blender into a bowl and repeat with the remaining soup and 1 cup rice milk. Transfer the puréed soup back into the saucepan and add the reserved cabbage, stirring to incorporate. Thin the soup if necessary by adding a little more rice milk, $^{1}/_{4}$ cup at a time, until the desired consistency is achieved. Taste and correct the seasoning. Reheat over low heat, stirring occasionally, until hot, taking care not to boil the soup.

Fish and Shellfish

Many supermarkets now have extensive offerings within their seafood department, making fresh fish an integral part of our diets. This chapter offers recipes ranging from simple, everyday fare to casual elegance, using a wonderful selection of fish and shellfish. Although the technique for freezing fish has come a long way, nothing can replace the taste and texture of freshly caught fish. For this reason, all of the recipes in this chapter were prepared with fresh fish and shellfish. To maintain optimum freshness, always keep your fish or shellfish refrigerated, and plan to prepare it the same day or within 24 hours of purchasing it.

Salmon in Puff Pastry

Coconut-Lime Seafood Stew

Mahi Mahi with White Beans and Sundried Tomato Cream

Halibut in Swiss Chard Wraps

Roasted Hot and Spicy Crab

Sturgeon with Olive Tapenade

Seared Scallops in Asparagus Cream

Pecan-Crusted Trout

Asian Linguine and Clams

Seafood Pizza Tart

Garlic Prawns

Salmon in Puff Pastry

Wrapped in a delicate, golden brown pastry, the salmon and mushroom filling offer moist and tender flavors. This main course creates an elegant presentation, perfect for a special evening or holiday dinner.

Salmon Pastries

2 tablespoons olive oil

1 large yellow onion, finely chopped

3/4 pound mushrooms, thinly sliced

1 red bell pepper, seeded, deribbed, and finely chopped

3 tablespoons minced fresh tarragon

2 tablespoons sake

4 teaspoons freshly squeezed lemon juice

1/2 teaspoon salt

1/4 teaspoon freshly ground black pepper

2 tablespoons pareve mayonnaise

1 (17.3-ounce) package frozen puff pastry (2 sheets), thawed

4 (6-ounce) skinless, boneless fresh salmon fillets, each about 3/4 inch thick

1 large egg, beaten

......

Sauce

2 tablespoons pareve margarine

1 tablespoon flour

3/4 cup rice milk or soy milk

......

Tarragon sprigs for garnish (optional)

To prepare the filling: Heat the olive oil in a large skillet over medium-high heat, and sauté the onion until soft, 3 to 4 minutes. Add the mushrooms and sauté until their liquid has evaporated, about 8 minutes. Add the bell pepper, 2 tablespoons of the tarragon, 1 tablespoon of the sake, 2 teaspoons of the lemon juice, and the salt, and pepper, and continue to sauté until the liquid has evaporated, about 3 minutes. Transfer the filling to a bowl and allow it to cool for about 30 minutes. Fold the mayonnaise into the cool filling until incorporated.

To assemble the pastries: Preheat the oven to 425°. Lightly oil a baking sheet. On a lightly floured surface, roll out each puff pastry sheet to 12 by 13 inches, and cut 1 inch off each sheet to form a 12-inch square. Reserve the 1-inch strips for decoration. Cut each square in half, forming four 12 by 6-inch rectangles. On each rectangle, place one salmon fillet about 4 inches from one short edge and centered. Spoon the filling equally over the salmon, using all of the filling. Using a pastry brush, brush the edges of each pastry rectangle with egg. Take the short end of the pastry opposite the salmon, and fold it over the filling. Continue to roll up the pastry until the salmon is fully enclosed. With your fingers, pinch the edges of the pastry closed, and then fold the edges under. Place the pastries seam side down on the prepared baking sheet.

To decorate the pastry: Braid or twist the remaining strips of pasty dough and replace them on top of the pastries. Or use canapé cutters to cut out various shapes for the top. Brush the top and sides of the pastries with egg, and bake until golden brown, about 20 minutes. Remove from the oven and let stand 5 minutes before serving.

To prepare the sauce: Melt the margarine in a small saucepan over low heat. Whisk in the flour until incorporated. Whisk in the remaining 1 tablespoon tarragon, 1 tablespoon sake, and 2 teaspoons lemon juice until blended and smooth. Bring to a boil and cook for 1 minute, then decrease the heat to low and whisk in the rice milk until smooth, about 2 minutes. The sauce will be thin. Spoon the sauce onto plates and place the pastries on top of the sauce. Garnish each plate with sprigs of tarragon.

Coconut-Lime Seafood Stew

Without question, this is my father's favorite dish. And no wonder—it's loaded with fresh seafood, has a rich and creamy broth, and is altogether deeply satisfying. The turmeric gives the broth a lovely golden hue with lemon undertones and makes the dish shine. Serve it with lots of crusty French bread.

2 tablespoons olive oil

1 large yellow onion, chopped

1 tablespoon peeled, minced fresh ginger, or 1 teaspoon ground ginger

1 teaspoon ground turmeric

1 (8-ounce) bottle clam juice

1 (14-ounce) can unsweetened coconut milk

2 cups chopped tomatoes with their juice (page 166)

1³/4 pounds new red potatoes, cut into 1-inch pieces

1 teaspoon grated lime zest

¹/2 teaspoon salt

¹/4 teaspoon freshly ground black pepper

1 cup whole fresh basil leaves, stemmed and tightly packed

1 pound fresh littleneck clams or mussels, scrubbed

¹/2 pound fresh skinless, boneless halibut steak, cut into 1-inch cubes

¹/2 pound fresh jumbo prawns, deveined

¹/2 pound fresh jumbo scallops

2 tablespoons freshly squeezed lime juice (1 to 2 limes)

Lime wedges for garnish (optional)

To prepare the stew: Heat the olive oil in a large, heavy saucepan over medium-high heat. Add the onion and sauté until tender, about 3 minutes. Stir in the ginger and turmeric until blended, about 1 minute. Stir in the clam juice, coconut milk, tomatoes, potatoes, lime zest, salt, and pepper. Bring to a boil. Cover, decrease the heat to low, and simmer for 18 to 20 minutes, stirring occasionally. Add the basil and clams, and continue simmering until the clams open, 5 to 7 minutes. Discard any that do not open. Add the halibut, prawns, scallops, and lime juice and stir until incorporated. Cover and simmer until just heated through, 2 to 3 minutes. Taste and correct the seasonings. Ladle into bowls, garnish each with a lime wedge, and serve immediately.

Note: When you purchase live mollusks (shellfish) from the market, it is important to remove them from the plastic bag as soon as you get home. Store them in the refrigerator in a bowl with about ¹/4 inch of water and a wet paper towel draped over the top of the bowl. This simple procedure will ensure that your mollusks remain fresh until you are ready to use them.

Mahi Mahi with White Beans and Sundried Tomato Cream

1/4 cup olive oil

1 large yellow onion, coarsely
 chopped

1 cup chopped carrot (about
 2 medium)

1 cup chopped celery (about
 3 stalks)

3 cloves garlic

6 fresh sage leaves, chopped

2 sprigs winter savory or thyme

1 bay leaf

1 tablespoon grated lemon zest
 (2 to 3 lemons)

1/4 cup dry white wine

2 cups cooked white beans or
 Great Northern beans
 (page 170)

1/2 cup chopped tomatoes with
 their juice (page 166)

1/2 cup chicken stock (page 164)

1/2 teaspoon salt

1/4 teaspoon freshly ground black
 pepper

4 (6-ounce) mahi mahi steaks,
 3/4 to 1 inch thick

3/4 cup Sundried Tomato Cream
 (page 115)

Lemon wedges for garnish
 (optional)

This dish has three components—beans, fish, and sauce—and together they make a wonderful meal. If you cook the beans ahead of time or use canned beans, you can assemble this entrée in just minutes. The sauce can be prepared the day before and rewarmed while the fish is cooking. You can use any firm whitefish in this recipe, including halibut or sturgeon.

To prepare the beans: Heat 2 tablespoons of the olive oil in a large, heavy saucepan over medium-high heat and sauté the onion, carrot, celery, and garlic until just tender, about 5 minutes. Add the sage, savory, bay leaf, zest, and wine; stir for 1 minute. Add the beans, tomatoes, chicken stock, salt, and pepper and toss to combine all ingredients. Cover and simmer until just heated through, about 15 minutes. Remove from the heat and cover to keep warm.

To prepare the fish: Heat the remaining 2 tablespoons of olive oil in a large skillet over medium-high heat until hot. Lightly salt and pepper the mahi mahi. Place the fish in the hot skillet, partially covering the skillet with a lid to lessen the splattering. Cook for 4 to 5 minutes. Flip the fish over and continue to cook the other side until lightly browned, 3 to 4 minutes.

To serve, spoon the beans onto the center of each plate and place the mahi mahi on top of the beans. Spoon about 2 tablespoons of the Sundried Tomato Cream on top, and serve immediately.

Halibut in Swiss Chard Wraps

These tasty little packages make a nice presentation for an Easter supper or special weekend dinner. Some time ago, I made this dish for our friends the Floreani's; they enjoyed it so much, they often ask about having it again! If you prefer, substitute New Zealand cod (Hoki) or striped bass for the halibut.

Filling

1 (8-ounce) bottle clam juice
1 1/2 ounces dry-packed sundried
    tomatoes (about 3/4 cup)
4 cloves garlic, minced
2 tablespoons olive oil

1/4 teaspoon dried lemongrass
1/2 teaspoon salt
1/4 teaspoon freshly ground black
    pepper

. . . . . .

Wraps

8 large Swiss chard leaves, thick
    stems removed
4 (8-ounce) skinless, boneless fresh
    halibut fillets, each about 1 1/2
    inches thick and 2 inches wide

. . . . . .

Sauce

3 tablespoons pareve margarine
5 tablespoons flour
1 teaspoon freshly squeezed lemon
    juice

1/4 cup dry sherry
3/4 cup rice milk or soy milk
4 thin slices lemon for garnish
    (optional)

To prepare the filling: Combine the clam juice and tomatoes in a small covered saucepan over medium-high heat, bring to a boil, and boil for 2 minutes. Remove the saucepan from the heat and allow it to sit, covered, for 15 minutes.

With a slotted spoon, transfer the tomatoes to a cutting board and mince. Reserve the clam juice for later. Combine the tomatoes, garlic, olive oil, lemongrass, salt, and pepper in a small bowl, and stir to blend.

To prepare the chard and assemble the wraps: Place a large pot fitted with a steaming basket and water over medium-high heat, and bring to a boil. Place the chard in the basket and steam until just wilted, about 30 seconds. Remove the basket and rinse the chard under cold running water; drain well.

Place one chard leaf on a wide, flat working surface. Place another leaf next to the first, overlapping the long sides, and pat the chard dry with a paper towel. Place one fish fillet crosswise near the end of the chard. Take about 1 teaspoon of the tomato mixture and spread it evenly over the fillet. Fold the two long sides of the chard over the fish, rolling the fish up in the chard and enclosing it completely. Repeat the process with the remaining chard and fish. Place the wrapped fillets seam side down in an 8 by 11 by 2-inch baking dish. The wraps can be made 1 day ahead. Cover and refrigerate.

To prepare the sauce and bake the wraps: Preheat the oven to 350°. Melt the margarine in a small saucepan over low heat. Whisk in the flour, a little at a time, until incorporated. Add the reserved clam juice, bring to a boil, and cook for 2 minutes, whisking until smooth. Whisk in the lemon juice, sherry, and rice milk until incorporated. The sauce will be thick but will thin while baking. Pour the sauce over the wraps, cover with aluminum foil, and bake for 40 to 45 minutes. Spoon the sauce onto a plate and place a wrap on top of the sauce. Garnish each wrap with a slice of lemon.

Roasted Hot and Spicy Crab

Serves 4

I love to serve this crab for dinner on New Year's Eve, when lingering over a meal is a treat. Serve it in front of a crackling fire with a tossed green salad, French bread, and plenty of champagne.

$^1/_3$ cup pareve margarine

$^1/_3$ cup extra virgin olive oil

3 tablespoons minced garlic (6 to 9 cloves)

2 tablespoons peeled, minced fresh ginger

2 tablespoons minced red onion

3 tablespoons freshly squeezed lemon juice (1 to 2 lemons)

2 teaspoons chili powder

1 tablespoon hot pepper sauce

1 teaspoon sugar

$^1/_4$ teaspoon crushed red pepper flakes, more or less to taste

5 Dungeness crabs, cooked, cleaned, and cracked (about 6 pounds total)

Lemon wedges for garnish (optional)

To make the marinade: Melt the margarine and olive oil in a large saucepan over medium-high heat. Sauté the garlic, ginger, and onion for about 1 minute. Add the lemon juice, chili powder, hot pepper sauce, sugar, and pepper flakes, and stir until the marinade is well blended and the sugar has dissolved, about 2 minutes. Remove the saucepan from the heat and allow the mixture to cool slightly, about 5 minutes.

To marinate the crab: Place the crab in a large bowl or heavy self-sealing plastic bag, pour the marinade over the crab, and toss to coat all pieces thoroughly. Cover and refrigerate for 1 to 3 hours, turning the crab occasionally.

To roast the crab: Preheat the oven to 500°. In a heavy 12 by 16-inch roasting pan, place the crab and marinade. Roast the crab, uncovered, until garlic is golden brown and the crab is hot, 10 to 15 minutes. Arrange the crab on a platter and garnish with lemon wedges.

Sturgeon with Olive Tapenade

Serves 4

$^1/_4$ cup bread crumbs (page 174)

$^1/_2$ cup Olive Anchovy Tapenade
(page 29)

3 tablespoons olive oil

1 teaspoon dry white wine

1 teaspoon freshly squeezed lemon
juice

$^1/_4$ teaspoon salt

$^1/_8$ teaspoon freshly ground black
pepper

4 (6-ounce) sturgeon fillets, about
1 inch thick

Lemon wedges for garnish
(optional)

To prepare the tapenade: Combine the bread crumbs, tapenade, 1 table-spoon of the olive oil, wine, and lemon juice in a small bowl. Stir until well combined.

To prepare the fish: Preheat the oven to 400°. Heat the remaining 2 table-spoons olive oil in a large skillet over medium-high heat until very hot. Lightly salt and pepper the sturgeon. Place the fillets in the hot skillet, partially covering the skillet with a lid to lessen the splattering. Sear the sturgeon until golden brown, about 3 minutes. Flip the fish over and sear the other side for about 3 minutes. Transfer the fillets to a baking dish and place them side by side in a single layer. Spoon 2 tablespoons of the tapenade atop each fish fillet. Bake the fish, uncovered, until opaque in the center, 10 to 12 minutes. Transfer to individual plates, and garnish with a lemon wedge. Serve immediately.

Simple and delicious best describes this recipe. The delicate flavor of the sturgeon marries beautifully with the Mediterranean trilogy of olives, capers, and anchovies found in the tapenade. Sturgeon is usually readily available, but you can substitute striped bass, halibut, or mahi mahi.

Seared Scallops in Asparagus Cream

Delicate yet flavorful, this dish is special enough for a dinner party or a romantic Valentine's Day dinner. I enjoy using fresh fettuccine noodles for this dish, but if they are not available, dried noodles work equally well. Serve with a light citrus salad such as Mixed Greens with Citrus and Candied Pecans (page 37).

1 pound asparagus spears
2 cups chicken stock (page 164)
1 large yellow onion, coarsely chopped
$1/2$ cup dry white wine
2 tablespoons pareve margarine
2 tablespoons flour
1 (12-ounce) package dried fettuccine noodles, or 1 pound fresh
1 pound fresh jumbo scallops (3 per person, 12 in all)
Salt
Freshly cracked pepper
2 tablespoons olive oil

$1/3$ pound mushrooms, thinly sliced
1 red bell pepper, seeded, deribbed, and julienned
10 fresh basil leaves, hand torn
4 ounces smoked salmon, cut into 2-inch pieces
1 teaspoon freshly squeezed lemon juice
$1/4$ teaspoon salt
1/8 teaspoon freshly ground black pepper
Grated lemon zest for garnish (optional)

To prepare the sauce: Trim the ends from the asparagus and cut the stems diagonally into 1-inch pieces, leaving the tips 3 inches long. Combine the chicken stock, onion, white wine, and asparagus stems, reserving the tips for later, in a saucepan, and bring to a boil. Cover, decrease the heat to low, and simmer until the vegetables are tender, 25 to 30 minutes. Remove the saucepan from the heat and let cool slightly. Ladle the mixture into a blender, and purée until smooth.

Melt the margarine in a large saucepan over medium-low heat. Whisk in the flour and cook for about 1 minute; do not brown. Pour the puréed mixture into the saucepan and whisk until the sauce begins to thicken, about 4 minutes. Remove the saucepan from the heat and set aside. Allow the sauce to cool. If preparing ahead, cover and refrigerate. The sauce can be made 1 day ahead.

Cook the fettuccine noodles according to the package directions. Drain and rinse under warm running water, and then drain again.

To sear the scallops: Pat the scallops dry with a paper towel and season lightly with salt and freshly cracked pepper. Heat 1 tablespoon of the olive oil in a large nonstick skillet over medium-high heat. Add the scallops to the hot skillet and sear on all sides for 3 to 4 minutes. Do not overcook the scallops, or they will become tough. Transfer them to a bowl, cover, and set aside.

⌒**To complete the sauce and assemble the dish:** Cut the asparagus tips diagonally into $1^1/_2$-inch pieces. In the same large skillet, heat the remaining 1 tablespoon olive oil over medium-high heat and sauté the mushrooms, bell pepper, basil, and asparagus tips for 2 to 3 minutes. Do not drain off the liquid. Stir in the puréed mixture and bring to a boil. Decrease the heat to low and add the salmon, lemon juice, salt, and pepper. Simmer for about 3 minutes, stirring occasionally. Serve in large individual bowls, ladling the sauce over the noodles and placing 3 scallops on top of each serving. Garnish with lemon zest and serve immediately.

Pecan-Crusted Trout

The rich and crunchy
texture of the pecans
provides a nice contrast
to the light and flaky trout,
resulting in fish that is
crisp on the outside and
moist inside. To give this
recipe a Southern flair,
add more cayenne pepper
and use catfish in place of
the trout.

1 cup bread crumbs (page 174)
1/2 cup finely chopped pecans
1/2 teaspoon salt
1/2 teaspoon chili powder
1/4 teaspoon cayenne pepper
2 tablespoons pareve margarine
2 cloves garlic, minced

4 (10- to 12-ounce) whole trout,
  butterflied and boned, with
  skin
2 tablespoons vegetable oil
Lemon wedges for garnish
  (optional)

Preheat the oven to 400°.

To prepare the fish: Combine the bread crumbs, pecans, salt, chili powder, and cayenne in a small bowl, and stir to blend. Melt the margarine in a small saucepan over medium heat. Add the garlic and sauté for 1 minute. Open the trout and place them skin side down on a large baking sheet; brush with the garlic butter. Coat the trout with the nut mixture, pressing it to help it adhere.

Heat 1 tablespoon of the oil in a large, nonstick skillet over medium-high heat until hot. Place 2 trout, nut side down, into the hot skillet, and cook for about 2 minutes. Using a spatula, flip the trout over and transfer to the baking sheet, nut side up. Repeat with the remaining 1 tablespoon of oil and trout. Bake the trout, uncovered, until just opaque in the center, 4 to 5 minutes.

Transfer to individual plates and garnish with a lemon wedge. Serve immediately.

Asian Linguine and Clams

1 (16-ounce) package dried
    linguine
3 tablespoons sesame oil
1 large yellow onion, finely
    chopped
1 red bell pepper, seeded, deribbed,
    and julienned
1¹/₂ tablespoons peeled, minced
    fresh ginger
2 cloves garlic, minced
1 seeded, minced jalapeño pepper,
    more or less to taste

1 (8-ounce) bottle clam juice
¹/₂ cup water
3 tablespoons rice vinegar
3 tablespoons sake
2 tablespoons soy sauce
32 fresh littleneck clams, scrubbed
¹/₄ cup thinly sliced green onion,
    both white and green parts
¹/₄ cup chopped fresh cilantro

To prepare the pasta: Bring 3 quarts of water to a boil in a large saucepan over high heat. Add the linguine to the water, bring to a boil, and stir. Cook the linguine, uncovered, according to the package directions, taking care not to overcook it. Drain the linguine in a colander and allow it to cool slightly. Transfer to a large bowl and toss with 1 tablespoon of the sesame oil to coat.

To prepare the dish: In the same large saucepan, heat the remaining 2 tablespoons of sesame oil over medium-high heat. Add the onion, bell pepper, ginger, garlic, and jalapeño, stirring frequently. Sauté until the vegetables begin to soften, about 5 minutes. Add the clam juice, water, vinegar, sake, and soy sauce. Bring to a boil. Add the clams and green onion. Cover and cook until the clams open, 5 to 7 minutes, discarding any that do not open. Taste and correct the seasonings. Spoon the clams and sauce over the pasta, sprinkle with cilantro, and serve.

Ingredients such as ginger, sesame oil, cilantro, and soy sauce add an Asian spin to classic linguine and clams, making this dish an aromatic delight for the senses. Be sure to use fresh ginger, as dried will not offer the desired flavor in this recipe. Jalapeño peppers can vary in the amount of heat they put out, from medium to very hot. Be sure you try a little taste before adding it to the dish.

Seafood Pizza Tart

Crust

1¹/₄ cups flour

2 teaspoons minced fresh thyme

¹/₄ cup pareve margarine

2 tablespoons olive oil

2 tablespoons rice milk or soy milk

......

Sauce

1 tablespoon olive oil

3 cloves garlic, minced

2 cups chopped tomatoes
  (page 166)

......

Topping

¹/₂ small globe eggplant, cut
  lengthwise

2 tablespoons olive oil

¹/₄ pound fresh rock shrimp

¹/₄ pound fresh bay scallops

In Provence, France, they make a pizza crust without yeast, more like a tart shell, and top it with niçoise olives and anchovies. In Naples, Italy, they make a yeast pizza crust that is thin, light, and crisp. Often it's simply topped with a delicate but flavorful tomato sauce and seasonal toppings. Both pizza styles are unique and quite delicious. This recipe combines these two styles and is dairy-free. After you have tried the seafood version, experiment with your favorite toppings.

↪**To make crust:** Combine the flour and thyme in a bowl and mix together with a wire whisk to blend. Add the margarine and olive oil and crumble the mixture through your fingers until it resembles coarse sand. Add the rice milk and mix quickly with your hands, gathering the dough into a ball. Flatten the dough into a disk, taking care not to overwork the dough. Wrap in plastic wrap and refrigerate for at least 2 hours.

↪**To prepare the sauce:** Heat the olive oil in a saucepan over medium-high heat, and sauté the garlic for about 1 minute. Add the tomatoes and bring to a boil. Decrease the heat to medium-low and simmer the tomatoes, uncovered, until they are reduced to ³/₄ cup, about 20 minutes. Remove from the heat and set aside to cool slightly.

↪**To prepare the topping:** Slice the eggplant half lengthwise into three ¹/₄-inch-thick pieces. Lightly sprinkle with salt and place the slices on paper towels to drain for about 30 minutes. Change the towels and blot the eggplant occasionally. Heat 1 tablespoon of the olive oil in a large skillet over medium-high heat. Add the eggplant to the skillet and sauté until softened, 6 to 8 minutes. Transfer to a cutting board and slice the eggplant lengthwise into strips about 1 inch thick. Set aside. Combine the shrimp and scallops with the remaining 1 tablespoon olive oil in a small bowl, tossing to coat. Set aside.

⌒**To assemble and bake the pizza:** Preheat the oven to 425°. Lightly oil a baking sheet. Place the dough between 2 sheets of plastic wrap. Using a rolling pin, roll out the dough to form a circle 11 to 12 inches in diameter, periodically lifting and repositioning the plastic wrap over the dough. Remove the plastic wrap and place the dough on the baking sheet. Crimp the edges of the dough to form a stand-up border. Spread the sauce evenly over the dough. Distribute the eggplant over the sauce. Using a slotted spoon, lift the seafood from the oil, reserving the oil. Arrange the shrimp and scallops randomly but evenly over the top. Lightly brush the reserved oil over the top and around the crust. Bake the pizza until the crust is crisp and golden, about 20 minutes. Remove from the oven and let stand for 5 minutes. Transfer to a platter, cut, and serve.

Garlic Prawns

Delicious and easy to prepare, this dish makes a colorful and sophisticated entrée, or the recipe can be halved and served as a starter. Serve these garlic-infused prawns simply, with basmati or jasmine rice and your favorite sautéed greens.

4 tablespoons pareve margarine
2 tablespoons olive oil
6 cloves garlic, minced
1 ¹/₂ pounds fresh jumbo prawns peeled, and deveined (8 per person, 32 in all)
¹/₃ cup dry white wine

2 tablespoons freshly squeezed lemon juice
2 tablespoons capers, drained
2 tablespoons minced fresh flat-leaf parsley
Lemon wedges for garnish (optional)

To prepare the prawns: Melt the margarine with the olive oil in a large sauté pan over medium-high heat. Add the garlic and sauté for 1 minute. Add the prawns and sauté for 2 minutes. Add the wine, lemon juice, and capers, and continue to sauté the prawns until just opaque in the center, about 2 to 3 minutes. Take care not to overcook the prawns or they will become tough. Remove the pan from the heat and toss with the parsley. Transfer the prawns to individual plates, spoon the sauce over the top, and garnish with a wedge of lemon. Serve immediately.

Poultry and Meat

From everyday family favorites, such as Manicotti Florentine, to a Thanksgiving Herb-Roasted Turkey, these main courses offer a wide variety of options. The recipes in this chapter primarily use poultry, but most of them can also be prepared with beef, pork, or lamb. Two such examples are the Sweet Basil Turkey Loaf with Mushroom Sauce (page 72) and the Smoked Sausage Spinach Risotto (page 73).

Sweet Basil Turkey Loaf with Mushroom Sauce

Nothing quite says comfort food like meat loaf smothered in creamy sauce, served with mashed potatoes. This turkey loaf makes a great casual weeknight dinner as well as terrific sandwiches the following day. It's a snap to prepare and can easily be assembled the night before. Extra-lean ground beef, ground lamb, or a combination of the two work equally well; just be sure to drain off the excess fat once the loaf is pulled from the oven.

$1^1/_4$ pounds ground turkey
$^1/_2$ pound carrots, peeled and
　　minced or grated
1 large yellow onion, minced
2 cloves garlic, minced
1 red bell pepper, seeded, deribbed,
　　and minced
$^3/_4$ cup stemmed and coarsely
　　chopped fresh basil

1 cup quick oats
1 large egg
$^1/_4$ cup cream sherry
$^1/_4$ teaspoon salt
$^1/_4$ teaspoon freshly ground black
　　pepper
Mushroom Sauce (page 117)

To prepare and bake the turkey loaf: Preheat the oven to 350°. Place the turkey, carrots, onion, garlic, bell pepper, basil, oats, egg, sherry, salt, and pepper in a large bowl. With well-washed hands, mix the ingredients together until well combined. Pat the mixture into an $8^1/_2$ by $4^1/_2$ by $2^1/_2$-inch loaf pan and bake until lightly browned and the juices run clear, $1^1/_2$ hours.

To serve the loaf: Allow the loaf to rest in the pan about 15 minutes before slicing. Slice the turkey loaf into $^3/_4$-inch-thick slices, and ladle the Mushroom Sauce on top. Serve immediately.

Smoked Sausage Spinach Risotto

5 tablespoons olive oil

2 cups precooked smoked chicken sausage (about $^1/_2$ pound), thinly sliced

2 cloves garlic, minced

6 ounces fresh baby spinach, stemmed (about $^1/_2$ bunch)

$^1/_4$ cup pareve margarine

1 large yellow onion, finely chopped

2 cups arborio rice

$1^1/_4$ cups dry white wine

6 cups chicken stock (page 164)

$^1/_2$ teaspoon salt

$^1/_4$ teaspoon freshly ground black pepper

To prepare the sausage mixture: Heat 3 tablespoons of the olive oil in a large skillet over medium-high heat, and sauté the sausage, garlic, and spinach until the spinach is wilted, about 3 minutes; set aside.

To cook the risotto: Melt the margarine with the remaining 2 tablespoons olive oil in a large saucepan over medium heat. Sauté the onion until soft and golden, about 8 minutes. Add the rice to the oil mixture and, using a wooden spoon, toss to coat the rice thoroughly. Stir in the wine $^1/_2$ cup at a time until it has been absorbed, reserving $^1/_4$ cup of wine for later use. Add the chicken stock to the rice mixture, a ladleful at a time, stirring constantly after each addition until the liquid has been absorbed. Continue adding the stock, a ladleful at a time, until a creamy sauce has developed and all of the remaining stock has been used; this should take about 20 minutes. Add the sausage mixture with its juices and the last $^1/_4$ cup of wine, stirring until the wine has been absorbed and the risotto is creamy, about 5 minutes. Taste and correct the seasoning. The total cooking time for the rice is approximately 25 minutes. Serve immediately.

Italian in origin, risotto can be served as a main course or side dish. Many supermarkets carry an assortment of chicken and turkey sausages, my favorites being Aidells Smoked Chicken & Apple sausage and Smoked Turkey & Chicken Artichoke with Roasted Garlic sausage. You can also make this recipe using pork sausage, provided you have cooked the pork completely before adding it to the garlic and spinach mixture.

Peppered Pork Tenderloin in Mustard Cream Sauce

The searing process used in this recipe produces a delightful crusty pork tenderloin with a subtle infusion of pepper. Mixed peppercorns—red, green, white, and black—can be found in the spice section of your local supermarket. Serve the pork alongside Scalloped Potatoes (page 92) and Lemon Garlic Crusted Leeks (page 103).

3 tablespoons mixed peppercorns
2 pork tenderloins, trimmed
    (about 2 pounds total)

$^1/_2$ teaspoon salt
2 tablespoons olive oil
Mustard Cream Sauce (page 117)

To prepare the pork: Coarsely grind the peppercorns in a blender or spice grinder. Lightly sprinkle the pork with salt. Press the pepper onto the pork, coating it completely. Heat the olive oil in a large sauté pan over medium-high heat until hot. Place the pork tenderloins in the hot skillet, partially covering the skillet with a lid to lessen the splattering. Brown the pork on all sides and cook until an instant-read meat thermometer inserted into the thickest portion of the meat registers 150°, 15 to 20 minutes.

Transfer the pork to a cutting board and allow it to rest for 5 minutes. The temperature will continue to rise as it rests. Cut the pork into 1-inch-thick slices. Spoon the sauce onto individual plates and top with the pork.

Chicken Vera Cruz

1 teaspoon garlic powder

$^1/_2$ teaspoon salt

$^1/_2$ teaspoon freshly ground black
pepper

$^1/_8$ teaspoon ground cumin

4 boneless, skinless chicken breast
halves, lightly pounded

1 cup Black Bean Sauce
(page 114)

2 ripe avocados, halved lengthwise,
peel and pit removed

Pico de Gallo (page 121)

To prepare the chicken: Preheat the grill to 350° (a medium-hot fire). In a small bowl, combine the garlic powder, salt, pepper, and cumin; stir to blend. Lightly sprinkle both sides of the chicken with the seasonings. Place the chicken on the hot grill and grill for 2 to 3 minutes, rotate the chicken once 45 degrees, to make cross-hatched grill marks, and grill for an additional 2 minutes. Turn the chicken over and repeat until it is cooked through, for a total of 8 to 10 minutes, or until the juices run clear.

To assemble the dish: Spoon about $^1/_4$ cup of the black bean sauce into the center of each individual shallow bowl or rimmed plate. Place a chicken breast in the center of each pool of sauce. Slice each avocado half into 5 equal pieces and fan them out on top of a chicken breast. Spoon Pico de Gallo salsa on top, and serve.

The flavors of this Latin-inspired entrée are fresh, warm, and inviting. It has several parts—the Black Bean Sauce, succulent chicken, and luscious avocado, all crowned with a zesty salsa. Begin by making the Black Bean Sauce, then continue with the other elements. If you cook, shock, and refrigerate the black beans the day before, the sauce will take minutes to assemble. Just remember to save the cooking liquid from the beans—you'll need it to make the sauce.

Chicken with Potato and Leek in Tarragon Cream

This French-inspired dish is quick to assemble and can easily be made a day ahead; just cover and refrigerate. If refrigerated, allow an additional 10 minutes of baking time. For a boost of calcium, serve it alongside your favorite steamed or sautéed dark greens, such as kale, bok choy, or collard greens.

1 tablespoon olive oil

4 boneless, skinless chicken breast halves, pounded to a thickness of $1/4$ inch

$1/2$ teaspoon salt

$1/4$ teaspoon freshly ground black pepper

6 tablespoons flour

2 medium Yukon Gold potatoes, unpeeled, sliced $1/8$ inch thick

2 large leeks, white and light green part only, julienned

12 slices lemon, cut $1/8$ inch thick

3 tablespoons pareve margarine

1 cup chicken stock (page 164)

$1/3$ cup dry white wine

$1/2$ cup rice milk or soy milk

1 tablespoon freshly squeezed lemon juice

$1/4$ cup minced fresh tarragon

2 cloves garlic, minced

Tarragon sprigs for garnish (optional)

Preheat the oven to 350°.

To prepare the dish: Heat the olive oil in a large skillet over medium-high heat. Lightly season the chicken with salt and pepper, then dust the chicken with 2 tablespoons of the flour. Place the chicken in the hot skillet and sear each side until just browned, about 2 minutes.

Remove the chicken from the skillet and place side by side in an 8 by 11 by 2-inch glass baking dish. Fan 5 slices of potato on top of each chicken breast. Next evenly arrange the leeks on top of the potatoes, and finish by fanning 3 slices of lemon on top of the leeks. Set aside.

To prepare the sauce: Melt the margarine in a saucepan over medium-low heat. Add the remaining $1/4$ cup flour and whisk to blend. Whisking constantly, gradually add the chicken stock until incorporated. Then add the wine, rice milk, lemon juice, tarragon, and garlic. Cook until the sauce begins to thicken, 5 to 6 minutes. Taste and correct the seasoning.

Pour the sauce slowly over the layered chicken. Cover with aluminum foil and bake until the sauce is bubbly, about 40 minutes. Remove the dish from the oven and let it stand, covered, for 5 minutes. Serve with remaining sauce and a tarragon sprig garnish.

Mediterranean Roast Chicken

Serves 4

1 (3¹/₂- to 6-pound) fresh whole
   roasting chicken, giblets
   removed
¹/₄ cup Mediterranean Rub
   (page 126)

¹/₂ medium yellow onion,
   quartered

To prepare the chicken: Rinse the chicken inside and out and pat dry with paper towels. Place the chicken on a rack in the roasting pan and let it stand at room temperature for 30 minutes. Position the oven rack in the bottom third of the oven and preheat the oven to 375°.

Starting at the neck end, loosen the skin around the breast meat by sliding your hand under the skin. Using your hand, spread 2 teaspoons of the herb mixture under the skin of the chicken, evenly covering the breast meat. Rub the remaining herb mixture over the outside skin of the chicken and in the main cavity. Place half an onion inside the main cavity and tuck the wing tips under the chicken.

Roast the chicken for about 1¹/₂ to 2 hours depending on the size of the bird, or until an instant-read thermometer inserted into the thickest part of the thigh, without touching the bone, registers 175°. Remove the pan from the oven and allow the chicken to rest for about 10 minutes before carving.

Note: There are countless ways to roast a chicken but this method is my favorite. Elevating the chicken on a rack in the roasting pan permits the heat to circulate around the chicken and guarantees a uniform, crispy, golden brown skin. To keep the bird moist, you need to let it rest uncovered before carving. This allows the juices to draw back into the meat instead of draining out when cut.

Whether I am preparing a hearty meal for my family or an elegant get-together with friends, succulent roast chicken is a staple in our home. For a classic family-style meal, pair the chicken with Garlic Mashed Potatoes (page 93) and the Roasted Vegetable Medley (page 105). Or for a dinner party, formalize the chicken by serving it with Corn Soufflé (page 100) and Creamed Spinach (page 102). Either way it's delicious.

Manicotti Florentine

This dairy-free version of manicotti uses ground turkey breast combined with spinach and tofu, resulting in a rich yet healthy pasta dish. Using freshly prepared Herbed Tomato Sauce makes the dish even more delectable. If you choose to substitute ground beef, select the leanest option available, and drain off any excess fat before adding the spinach and wine.

Filling

2 tablespoons olive oil

1 large yellow onion, finely chopped

1 pound ground turkey breast

3 cloves garlic, minced

1 tablespoon minced fresh basil, or $^1/_2$ teaspoon dried

1 tablespoon minced fresh thyme, or $^1/_2$ teaspoon dried

$^1/_2$ teaspoon salt

$^1/_4$ teaspoon freshly ground black pepper

1 pound fresh spinach, stemmed and coarsely chopped, or collard greens

$^1/_3$ cup dry white wine

1 (12-ounce) package medium or firm tofu, drained

2 large eggs

$^1/_2$ cup bread crumbs (page 174)

......

1 (8-ounce) package dried large manicotti

4 cups Herbed Tomato Sauce (page 167)

$^1/_2$ cup water

To prepare the filling: Heat the olive oil in a large skillet over medium-high heat and sauté the onion until tender, about 3 minutes. Add the turkey, garlic, basil, thyme, salt, and pepper and cook, stirring frequently, until the turkey is just brown, about 8 minutes. Decrease the heat to medium, and add the spinach and wine. Cover and continue cooking, stirring occasionally, about 4 minutes. Remove from the heat and allow to cool slightly, about 10 minutes.

Meanwhile, wrap the tofu in several layers of paper towels and lightly press out the excess moisture. Beat the eggs in a large bowl until just combined. Add the bread crumbs and crumble the tofu so that it resembles large-curd cottage cheese; fold it in with a spatula to blend. Add the turkey-spinach mixture and toss together.

To assemble and bake the dish: Cook the manicotti according to the package directions. It should still be slightly firm, since it will cook further in the oven. Drain, rinse under warm running water, and drain again.

Preheat oven to 375°. Mix 1 cup of the tomato sauce with the water. Pour this mixture into the bottom of a 9 by 13 by 2-inch glass baking dish. Stuff the cooked manicotti with the filling, being careful not to split the shells. (If a shell splits, place it seam side down in the baking dish.) Arrange the manicotti in a single layer in the baking dish. Pour the remaining 3 cups tomato sauce evenly over it. Sprinkle any remaining filling on top. Cover the dish with aluminum foil and bake until the sauce is bubbly, 25 to 30 minutes. Let stand, covered, for 10 minutes before serving.

Wild Mushroom Lasagna

The blending of various mushrooms, and herbs makes this a distinctive lasagna, with complex flavors, and textures that are so satisfying, you won't miss the cheese. This lasagna is truly a labor of love, and needs about an hour and a half to assemble.

Filling

4 tablespoons olive oil

2 large onions, finely chopped

1 pound ground turkey

5 cloves garlic, minced

1/4 cup minced fresh flat-leaf parsley

1 tablespoon minced fresh thyme, or 1 1/2 teaspoons dried

1/4 teaspoon salt, plus more for seasoning mushrooms

1/4 teaspoon freshly ground black pepper

1/2 pound fresh white mushrooms, thinly sliced

3/4 pound fresh portobello mushrooms, stems trimmed and the caps halved, and thinly sliced

1 pound fresh oyster mushrooms, sliced

1/3 cup red wine or port

Chopped parsley for garnish (optional)

......

Sauce

1/4 cup olive oil

1/4 cup pareve margarine

1 cup flour

3 3/4 cups warm rice milk or soy milk

1 (16-ounce) package lasagna noodles

1/8 teaspoon ground nutmeg

3 large eggs, beaten

1/4 teaspoon salt

......

1 (12-ounce) package firm tofu, drained

To prepare the filling: Heat 2 tablespoons of the olive oil in a large skillet over medium-high heat, and sauté the onion until tender, about 3 minutes. Add the turkey, garlic, parsley, thyme, 1/4 teaspoon of the salt, and pepper. Cook, stirring frequently, until the turkey is just brown, about 8 minutes. Transfer the mixture to a large bowl, and set aside. Meanwhile, drain the tofu.

Heat the remaining 2 tablespoons of olive oil in the same skillet over medium-high heat. Add the mushrooms and sprinkle lightly with salt. Sauté, stirring occasionally, until the liquid has evaporated, and the mushrooms begin to sear, about 15 minutes. Add the wine to deglaze the pan, and sauté until the wine has evaporated, 2 to 3 minutes. Remove from the heat and set aside. Taste and correct the seasonings.

⌒To prepare the sauce: Heat the margarine and olive oil in a large saucepan over low heat until the margarine has melted. Whisking constantly, add the flour and cook until it is incorporated and the roux is bubbling, about 1 minute. Whisk in the rice milk, $^1/_2$ cup at a time, until a smooth sauce develops and thickens, about 5 minutes, taking care not to boil the sauce. Remove from the heat, and allow the sauce to cool slightly. Whisk in the nutmeg, eggs, and $^1/_4$ teaspoon of salt until well blended.

Cook the lasagna noodles according to package directions in salted boiling water. The noodles should still be slightly firm, since they will cook further in the oven. Drain, rinse under warm running water, and drain again.

⌒To assemble the lasagna: Preheat the oven to 375°. Slice the tofu block into 8 thin slices, measuring about 4 by 3 inches, similar to sliced cheese.

Lightly coat a 9 by 13 by 2-inch baking dish with cooking spray. Ladle about $^1/_4$ cup of the sauce to the bottom of the dish and spread it out evenly. Cover with a layer of noodles, overlapping the edges slightly. Spread half of the meat mixture on top of the pasta along with about a $^1/_2$ cup of sauce, distributing it evenly. Cover with another layer of noodles and spread half the mushroom mixture on top of the pasta. Lay the sliced tofu on top of the mushrooms, then ladle about a $^1/_2$ cup of sauce on top of them. Cover with another layer of noodles, and distribute the remaining meat mixture evenly over the pasta, followed by about a $^1/_2$ cup of sauce. Finish with a final layer of noodles and the balance of the mushroom mixture and sauce, taking care to spread the sauce evenly to cover the corners. Cover the dish tightly with aluminum foil, bake for 30 minutes, uncover, and bake for an additional 20 minutes. Remove the lasagna from oven and let stand 15 minutes before slicing. Garnish with chopped parsley.

Curried Stuffed Zucchini

My summertime garden inspired this recipe, when once again the small zucchini seed I planted in the spring produced an abundance of zucchini to enjoy all summer long. The delicate nature of the couscous pairs nicely with the fresh vegetables and sweet currants. Once prepared, the colors, textures, and aromas make this dish a feast for the senses.

1 ¹/₂ pounds zucchini (4 medium to large)

......

Stuffing

1 tablespoon olive oil

1 large yellow onion, finely chopped

¹/₂ pound turkey sausage, casing removed and finely chopped (mild or spicy)

3 cloves garlic, minced

1 red bell pepper, seeded, deribbed, and finely chopped

¹/₂ cup finely chopped fresh cilantro (about 1 bunch)

¹/₄ cup dried currants

1 tablespoon fresh lemon juice

......

Sauce

¹/₂ cup rice milk or soy milk

1 tablespoon yellow curry powder

¹/₄ teaspoon salt

¹/₄ teaspoon freshly ground black pepper

......

4 cups cooked couscous

Lemon slices for garnish (optional)

Preheat the oven to 350°.

To prepare the zucchini: Trim the ends from the zucchini, and slice them in half lengthwise. Using a teaspoon and being careful not to break the outside skin, core out the center of the zucchini, leaving a ¹/₂-inch-thick shell and saving the removed pulp. Chop the removed pulp and set aside.

To prepare the stuffing: Heat the olive oil in a large skillet over medium-high heat and sauté the onion until soft, about 3 minutes. Add the sausage and garlic, and sauté until evenly browned, about 5 minutes. Add the bell pepper, cilantro, zucchini pulp, currants, and lemon juice. Cover and simmer for 2 to 3 minutes, stirring occasionally. Remove the skillet from the heat and set aside.

To stuff and bake the zucchini: Place the zucchini shells in a shallow baking dish, hollow side up and side by side. Using a slotted spoon, fill each zucchini shell with the stuffing, using all of the stuffing. Reserve the liquid in the skillet.

To prepare the sauce and bake the dish: Place the skillet with the reserved liquid over medium-high heat, and bring to a boil. Decrease the heat to low and whisk in the rice milk, curry powder, salt, and pepper. Whisking constantly, simmer the sauce until the curry powder has completely dissolved, 2 to 3 minutes. Spoon over the stuffed zucchini, and cover with aluminum foil. Bake the zucchini until tender, 25 to 30 minutes.

To serve, divide the couscous among 4 plates and place zucchini halves on top of the couscous. Spoon the sauce over the top. Garnish with a slice of lemon.

Stuffed Red Bell Peppers

6 large red bell peppers

Stuffing

2 tablespoons olive oil

*1 large yellow onion, finely
chopped*

3 sprigs thyme

³/₄ pound ground turkey

3 cloves garlic, minced

*¹/₂ pound white mushrooms,
thinly sliced*

*¹/₂ pound carrots, peeled and
finely chopped*

*3 cups chopped tomatoes
(page 166)*

*¹/₃ cup finely chopped fresh
flat-leaf parsley*

¹/₂ teaspoon salt

*¹/₄ teaspoon freshly ground black
pepper*

¹/₂ cup cooked wild rice

1 cup cooked long-grain white rice

I often double or triple this recipe when assorted red, yellow, and orange bell peppers are in season and freeze them for a later date. Stuffed peppers freeze beautifully and make a delicious quick dinner when time is short or when unexpected guests drop in. Serve them in a tomato sauce or, as we frequently do, simmer them in chicken stock, split them open, and enjoy a light and satisfying Mediterranean soup.

To prepare the peppers: Set a large stockpot filled three-quarters full with water over high heat and bring to a boil. Meanwhile, with a small, sharp paring knife cut a circle around the stem of each bell pepper about 2 inches in diameter. Carefully remove the stem, seeds, and ribs. Blanch the peppers in the boiling water, ensuring that they are fully submerged, for 6 to 8 minutes. The peppers should be tender but still firm, since they will cook further in the oven. Using a large slotted spoon, transfer the peppers to a cold water bath to stop the cooking. Invert the peppers and drain well.

To prepare the stuffing: Heat the olive oil in a large skillet over medium-high heat, and sauté the onion and thyme until soft, about 3 minutes. Add the turkey, garlic, mushrooms, carrots, parsley, salt, and pepper. Sauté, stirring occasionally, until evenly browned and the liquid from the mushrooms has evaporated, 10 to 12 minutes. Transfer the mixture to a large bowl, remove the thyme sprigs, and set aside to cool. Add the wild and white rice and toss to combine.

⌒ **To stuff and bake the peppers:** Preheat the oven to 350°. Carefully stuff each of the peppers with the stuffing, packing it in lightly as you go, taking special care not to split the peppers. Place the bell peppers side by side in an 8 by 11 by 2-inch baking dish. Spoon the tomatoes over the peppers, cover with aluminum foil, and bake for about 30 minutes. If frozen, bake for about 1 hour 15 minutes.

⌒ **To freeze the peppers:** Once the peppers are stuffed, wrap them individually with a piece of plastic wrap, then place them side by side in a large self-sealing plastic freezer bag and freeze for up to 4 months.

Shepherd's Pie

Shepherd's Pie is essentially lamb stew smothered in mashed potatoes and baked. It can just as easily be made using chicken or simply vegetables. If you cover the stew with puff pastry in place of the mashed potatoes, you can easily transform it into pot pie. I've suggested my favorite vegetables for this recipe, but any vegetables you have on hand will work fine.

Sauce

2 tablespoons pareve margarine

2 tablespoons olive oil

1 large yellow onion, coarsely chopped

1 teaspoon minced fresh thyme, or $^{1}/_{2}$ teaspoon dried

$^{1}/_{2}$ teaspoon minced fresh rosemary, or $^{1}/_{4}$ teaspoon dried

$^{1}/_{4}$ teaspoon salt

3 cloves garlic, minced

$^{1}/_{2}$ cup red wine

5 tablespoons flour

$1^{1}/_{2}$ cups rice milk or soy milk

2 tablespoons minced flat-leaf parsley

......

Filling

6 whole dried shiitake mushrooms

$^{3}/_{4}$ cup hot water

2 tablespoons olive oil

1 pound lean boneless lamb, cut into $1^{1}/_{2}$-inch cubes

$^{1}/_{2}$ teaspoon salt

$^{1}/_{4}$ teaspoon freshly ground black pepper

$^{1}/_{3}$ pound fresh mushrooms, quartered

2 large red bell peppers, seeded, deribbed, and coarsely chopped

$^{3}/_{4}$ pound carrots, peeled and cut into 1-inch pieces

$^{1}/_{2}$ pound brussels sprouts, trimmed and halved

$^{1}/_{2}$ cauliflower, broken into florets (about $1^{1}/_{2}$ cups)

......

$^{1}/_{2}$ recipe Herbed Mashers (page 95)

To prepare the sauce: Melt the margarine with the olive oil in a large saucepan over medium heat. Add the onion, thyme, rosemary, and salt and sauté until the onion is lightly browned, about 6 minutes. Stir in the garlic and wine and reduce the liquid by half, about 5 minutes. Whisking constantly, slowly add the flour and cook for about 1 minute. Gradually whisk in the rice milk, $^{1}/_{2}$ cup at a time, until a smooth sauce develops, about 3 minutes. The sauce will be thick; do not allow it to boil. Whisk in the parsley, and taste and correct the seasonings.

To prepare the filling: Place the dried mushrooms in a small bowl with the hot water. Allow the mushrooms to soak for 20 minutes, swishing occasionally to loosen any grit. Lift the mushrooms out of the water with a slotted spoon and slice them in halves. Using a fine sieve, strain the liquid over a small bowl to remove any sediment. Reserve the liquid and set aside.

To assemble the dish: Preheat the oven to 375°. Heat the olive oil in a large skillet over medium-high heat. Season the lamb with the salt and pepper and add it to the hot skillet. Sear the lamb on all sides until it is lightly browned, about 4 minutes. Add the fresh mushrooms, bell pepper, carrots, brussels sprouts, cauliflower, and the reserved mushroom liquid, and cook for 4 to 5 minutes. Add the shiitake mushrooms and slowly add the sauce, stirring until it is fully incorporated. Transfer the mixture to a 4- to 5-quart casserole dish. Spoon the mashed potatoes evenly over the lamb and vegetable mixture, and bake until the sauce is bubbly, 40 to 45 minutes. Remove from the oven and let stand at room temperature for 10 minutes before serving.

Herb-Roasted Turkey

Apple–Corn Bread Stuffing is my favorite part of the Thanksgiving feast, and it is especially delicious served directly from the bird. The technique of rubbing the turkey meat under the skin with herbs allows for the maximum infusion of flavor and keeps the herbs moist and fragrant. The same applies to the herbs in the stuffing. As the bird roasts, the sage and thyme permeate and flavor the bird from the inside out.

1 18- to 20-pound fresh turkey
2 tablespoons minced fresh sage
1 tablespoon minced fresh thyme
2 teaspoons minced fresh rosemary
$^1/_4$ cup pareve margarine, at room temperature

Apple–Corn Bread Stuffing (page 109)
2 cups chicken stock (page 164)
Creamy Giblet Gravy (page 118)

To prepare the turkey: Position the oven rack in the bottom third of the oven, and preheat the oven to 325°. Rinse the turkey inside and out and pat dry with paper towels. Place the turkey on a rack in the roasting pan. Mix the sage, thyme, and rosemary in a small bowl.

Starting at the neck end, loosen the skin around the breast meat by sliding your hand under the skin. Using your hand, spread the margarine and 2 teaspoons of the herb mixture under the skin, evenly covering the breast meat. Rub the remaining herb mixture over the outside skin of the turkey. Fill the neck and main body cavity loosely with the stuffing, since the stuffing will expand as the bird cooks. (Bake any additional stuffing separately.) Tuck the wing tips under the turkey, and tie the legs together loosely.

To roast the turkey: Roast the turkey for 1 hour, and then baste with the pan juices. Add the chicken stock to the pan and continue roasting the turkey. Baste the turkey every 30 minutes until an instant-read meat thermometer inserted into the thickest part of the thigh, without touching the bone, registers 180°, 3 to $3^1/_2$ hours. Check for doneness about 30 minutes before the total roasting time is reached. The stuffing should reach an internal temperature of 160°. If roasting the turkey unstuffed, decrease the roasting time by approximately 30 minutes.

Transfer the turkey from the oven to a large carving board. Remove the stuffing from the turkey immediately after roasting and transfer it to a large bowl. Add the separately baked stuffing to the bowl and gently stir to blend. Keep warm. Allow the turkey to rest before carving, about 15 minutes. Meanwhile, prepare the gravy.

Note: About 15 years ago, I switched from buying a commodity turkey for our Thanksgiving feast to ordering a free-range, naturally grown turkey, and what a delicious difference it made. Typically, free-range natural birds are more tender and juicy and have a better meat-to-bone ratio and less water and fat than commodity turkeys. They're fed a vegetarian diet, free of animal by-products, stimulants, hormones, and antibiotics, resulting in a moist and tender bird with a fantastic flavor. Be sure to order your fresh bird at least 2 weeks in advance of the big day.

Beef Stroganoff

You'll be hard pressed to notice a difference between this stroganoff and traditional stroganoff made with sour cream. For a lighter version of this classic dish, try preparing it using lean turkey breast in place of the beef.

2 tablespoons olive oil
1 large yellow onion, coarsely chopped
1 pound boneless lean beef, sliced into 1-inch strips
$1/2$ teaspoon salt
$1/4$ teaspoon freshly ground black pepper
$1/3$ cup dry white wine
$3/4$ pound fresh mushrooms, thinly sliced

1 teaspoon fresh thyme, or $1/2$ teaspoon dried
$1/4$ cup chopped fresh flat-leaf parsley
$1/8$ teaspoon ground nutmeg
Lean Sour Cream (page 123)
1 (12-ounce) package wide pasta

To prepare the stroganoff: Heat the olive oil in a large skillet over medium-high heat, and sauté the onion until golden brown, about 5 minutes. Add the beef and season with salt and pepper. Sauté until evenly browned, 3 to 4 minutes. Add the wine, mushrooms, thyme, 2 tablespoons of the parsley, and nutmeg. Decrease the heat to medium-low, cover, and simmer for about 10 minutes, stirring occasionally. Add the sour cream and stir to blend. Simmer the stroganoff, uncovered, for about 5 minutes, stirring the mixture often and taking care not to boil the sauce.

Cook the pasta according to the package directions. Drain, rinse under warm running water, and drain again.

Serve by placing the pasta on individual plates and spooning the stroganoff mixture on top. Garnish with the remaining 2 tablespoons chopped parsley.

Vegetarian and Companion Dishes

Not just "side dishes" anymore, these versatile accompaniments to a main course, when done in combination, are a meal in themselves. Many people are electing to cut back on the amount of meat in their diet, thereby increasing vegetables and grains at mealtime. In keeping with how we are eating today, several of the following recipes are substantial enough to stand alone, such as the Broiled Polenta with Vegetable Ragout (page 107) and the Portobello Barley Risotto (page 96), although they also make wonderful accompaniments to a main course. For a menu using these dishes, see the Autumn Vegan Supper (page 6), a collection of dishes that complement one another, offering a hearty, delicious dinner to serve to friends or family.

Scalloped Potatoes

2 tablespoons pareve margarine

2 medium yellow onions, thinly
   sliced

1 bay leaf

3 cloves garlic, minced

1 tablespoon flour

2 pounds russet potatoes, peeled
   and thinly sliced

1 large egg

$^3/_4$ cup chicken stock (page 164)

$^3/_4$ cup rice milk or soy milk

1 teaspoon salt

$^1/_2$ teaspoon ground nutmeg

$^1/_4$ teaspoon freshly ground black
   pepper

1/4 teaspoon paprika

Elegant and satisfying, these potatoes make a scrumptious addition to any meat or fish entrée. I particularly enjoy pairing them with the Peppered Pork Tenderloin in Mustard Cream Sauce (page 74) or the Halibut in Swiss Chard Wraps (page 60). Onions are slowly sautéed with bay to draw out the subtle flavor, then layered with thin slices of potato. A touch of nutmeg sweetens the delicate cream sauce.

Preheat oven to 425°.

⤷**To prepare the onions:** Melt the margarine in a large sauté pan over medium-low heat. Add the onion and bay leaf and sauté until the onion is lightly caramelized, about 12 minutes. Add the garlic and sauté for an additional 2 to 3 minutes. Discard the bay leaf, sprinkle the onion with the flour, and stir to blend. Set aside.

⤷**To assemble the dish:** Coat the inside of an 8 by 11 by 2-inch baking dish generously with 1 tablespoon pareve margarine. Place one-third of the potatoes in the prepared dish in a single layer, slightly overlapping the edges of the potatoes. Spread one-half of the onion mixture on top of the potatoes. Add another layer, using one-third of the potatoes and the remaining onions. For the final layer, evenly distribute the remaining potatoes on top of the onions.

In a large bowl, whisk together the egg, chicken stock, rice milk, salt, nutmeg, and pepper to blend. Pour this mixture over the potatoes to coat them completely. Using the back of a fork, lightly press down on the potatoes to compact the layers. Finish by sprinkling with the paprika. Bake the dish, uncovered, for 30 minutes. Decrease the oven temperature to 350° and continue baking until the top is golden brown and the potatoes are tender, 35 to 40 minutes. Remove from the oven and let stand 15 minutes before serving.

Garlic Mashed Potatoes

10 large cloves garlic, peeled

$^1/_4$ cup pareve margarine

4 pounds russet potatoes, peeled and quartered

$^3/_4$ teaspoon salt

About 1 cup warm rice milk or soy milk

1 tablespoon chopped fresh flat-leaf parsley

$^1/_8$ teaspoon freshly ground black pepper

To prepare the garlic margarine: Thinly slice 3 cloves of the garlic, reserving the remaining whole cloves for later use. Melt the margarine in a skillet over low heat. Add the sliced garlic, sauté until the garlic is tender, about 10 minutes, and set aside.

To prepare the potatoes: Set a large pot filled with the potatoes, the remaining 7 cloves of garlic, and $^1/_4$ teaspoon of the salt, along with enough water to cover the potatoes by 2 inches, over high heat. Bring the water to a boil and cook the potatoes until they break apart easily with a fork, about 30 minutes. Drain the liquid.

To mash the potatoes: Transfer the potatoes, garlic, and garlic margarine to a large, deep bowl. Using an electric mixer, whip the potatoes with $^1/_2$ cup of the rice milk until the garlic is mashed and incorporated. Gradually add more rice milk, a little at a time, until the desired consistency is achieved and the potatoes are fluffy. Add the parsley and season with the remaining $^1/_2$ teaspoon salt and the pepper. Taste and correct the seasonings. Serve hot.

There is nothing modest about the presence of garlic in these potatoes. Rice or soy milk gives the potatoes a rich flavor, but it can be a little tricky to work with if you're not familiar with how this type of milk reacts with heat. It's important to note that if you don't serve the potatoes immediately and you keep them warm for too long a time, the rice or soy milk will thin, leaving the potatoes soupy. If you'll be preparing these potatoes in advance, it's best to replace the rice or soy milk with chicken stock or to reserve some of the potato-cooking liquid and use it instead.

Sweet Potato–Parsnip Mash

Sweet with a slightly
earthy flavor, these root
vegetables offer a nice
change of pace from
classic mashed potatoes.
Serve them at a holiday
meal or as a weeknight
side dish with roast
chicken or pork or
grilled tofu.

2¹/₂ pounds garnet sweet potatoes,
* peeled, and cut into 2-inch*
* pieces*
1 pound parsnips, peeled, and cut
* into 2-inch pieces*

¹/₂ teaspoon salt
5 tablespoons pareve margarine, at
* room temperature*
¹/₈ teaspoon freshly ground black
* pepper*

To prepare the potatoes: Place the potatoes and parsnips in a large pot and
add enough water to cover them by 2 inches, along with ¹/₄ teaspoon of the salt.
Bring the water to a boil and cook the vegetables until they break apart easily
with a fork, 25 to 30 minutes. Place a colander over a bowl and drain the potatoes, catching and reserving the cooking liquid.

To mash the potatoes: Transfer the potatoes and parsnips to a large, deep
bowl. Using an electric mixer, add the margarine, 1 cup of the reserved cooking liquid, the remaining ¹/₄ teaspoon salt, and pepper, and whip until the
potatoes are fluffy. If needed, gradually add a little more of the cooking liquid,
about ¹/₄ cup at a time, until the desired consistency is achieved. Taste and correct the seasonings. Serve hot.

Herbed Mashers

1 teaspoon salt

1 cup stemmed, thinly sliced fresh
    basil leaves, tightly packed

$^1/_2$ cup stemmed, thinly sliced
    fresh spinach leaves, tightly
    packed

$^1/_4$ cup stemmed, chopped fresh
    flat-leaf parsley

4 pounds Yukon Gold or red new
    potatoes, quartered

$^1/_3$ cup pareve margarine, melted
    and cooled

$^1/_4$ cup olive oil

$^1/_8$ teaspoon freshly ground black
    pepper

$^1/_4$ cup minced fresh chives (about
    2 bunches)

These fragrant, light potatoes are not only rich in minerals but also big on taste. They make a colorful alternative to ordinary spuds and work well with fish, chicken, beef, or lamb. They also make an aromatic topping for the Shepherd's Pie (page 86).

To prepare the potatoes: Set a large pot with about 10 cups of water, or enough water to cover the potatoes by about 1 inch, along with $^1/_4$ teaspoon of the salt, over high heat. Bring the water to a boil. Place the basil, spinach, and parsley in a fine-mesh strainer, and blanch the greens in the boiling water for about 1 minute. Remove the strainer, and place it under cold running water to stop the cooking. Drain. Add the potatoes to the boiling water and cook until they break apart easily with a fork, 25 to 30 minutes. Place a colander over a bowl and drain the potatoes, catching the cooking liquid.

To mash the potatoes: Transfer the potatoes to a large deep bowl. Using an electric mixer, whip the potatoes until fluffy, adding the margarine, olive oil, the remaining $^3/_4$ teaspoon salt, pepper, and $1^3/_4$ cups of the reserved cooking liquid, $^1/_2$ cup at a time. If needed, gradually add a little more of the cooking liquid, about $^1/_4$ cup at a time, until the desired consistency is achieved. Stir in the chives. Taste and correct the seasonings. Serve hot.

Portobello Barley Risotto

The rich, full-bodied flavor of portobello mushrooms and the nutty texture of toasted barley give this dish an earthy appeal. For a simple variation, try tossing in $^{1}/_{3}$ cup lightly toasted pine nuts, sunflower seeds, or almonds before serving. If added any sooner, the nuts will absorb moisture and lose their crunch.

5 tablespoons olive oil

2 large Portobello mushrooms (about 6 ounces), thinly sliced into $1^{1}/_{2}$-inch strips

3 cloves garlic, minced

$^{1}/_{2}$ teaspoon salt

$^{1}/_{4}$ teaspoon freshly ground black pepper

1 cup pearl barley

3 tablespoons pareve margarine

1 large yellow onion, finely chopped

$^{1}/_{2}$ cup dry white wine

4 cups chicken stock (page 164)

3 sprigs thyme, or $^{1}/_{2}$ teaspoon dried

To prepare the mushrooms: Heat 3 tablespoons of the olive oil in a large skillet over medium-high heat and sauté the mushrooms, garlic, salt, and pepper, until the mushrooms are softened, about 3 minutes; set aside.

To prepare the risotto: Place the barley in a large saucepan over medium-high heat and cook, stirring frequently, until lightly toasted about 5 minutes. Transfer the barley to a bowl.

In the same saucepan, melt the margarine with the remaining 2 tablespoons oil, and sauté the onion until soft and golden, about 8 minutes. Add the barley to the oil mixture and toss to coat, using a wooden spoon. Stir in the wine, $1^{1}/_{2}$ cups of the chicken stock, and the thyme. Bring the mixture to a boil. Decrease the heat to medium-low and simmer until most of the liquid has been absorbed, stirring frequently, 5 to 7 minutes. Add the remaining $2^{1}/_{2}$ cups stock, 1 cup at a time, stirring frequently after each addition, until the liquid has been absorbed. Continue adding the stock and stirring, until the barley is tender and creamy but still slightly firm to the bite, about 45 minutes. Remove the thyme sprigs, and stir in the mushroom mixture with any juices that have accumulated. Taste and correct the seasonings. Serve immediately.

Wild Lemon Pilaf with Currants

3 cups water

²/₃ cup wild rice

2 tablespoons pareve margarine

1 pound leeks, white and pale
    green parts only, julienned

1¹/₃ cups basmati or jasmine rice

3³/₄ cups chicken stock (page 164)

¹/₄ cup freshly squeezed lemon
    juice (about 2 lemons)

1 tablespoon chopped lemon zest
    (2 to 3 lemons)

¹/₃ cup dried currants

¹/₂ teaspoon salt

¹/₄ teaspoon freshly ground black
    pepper

¹/₄ cup slivered almonds, toasted
    (page 175)

⮑**To prepare the wild rice:** Bring the water to a boil in a saucepan over medium-high heat. Add the wild rice. Decrease the heat to medium-low and simmer, uncovered, for about 15 minutes. Remove from the heat and drain, using a fine-mesh strainer. Rinse under warm running water and drain again.

⮑**To prepare the pilaf:** Melt the margarine in a large, heavy saucepan over medium-high heat. Add the leeks and sauté until just soft, about 3 minutes. Mix in the wild and basmati rice, tossing to coat. Stir in the chicken stock, lemon juice, zest, currants, salt, and pepper. Bring the mixture to a boil, stirring occasionally. Cover, decrease the heat to low, and simmer until the liquid is absorbed and the rice is tender, about 35 minutes. Mix in the almonds and serve.

With its buttery fragrance and subtle, almost nutty flavor, basmati rice pairs perfectly with the rich texture of wild rice. This pilaf recipe, infused with lemon and lightly sweetened with plump currants, is delicious alongside the Salmon in Puff Pastry (page 56).

Blackstrap Beans

Team these calcium-rich beans with barbecued dishes, or use them as a topping for baked potatoes. Blackstrap molasses is a good source of iron, calcium, and potassium. To make these beans vegetarian, simply omit the bacon, or lighten the flavor by using turkey bacon. If omitting the bacon or using turkey bacon, use 2 tablespoons of olive oil to sauté the onion, bell pepper, and garlic.

6 slices pork bacon or turkey
    bacon slices
2 large yellow onions, chopped
1 green bell pepper, seeded,
    deribbed, and coarsely chopped
3 cloves garlic, minced
1^3/$_4$ cups chopped tomatoes
    (page 166)
^{1}/$_2$ cup water
^{1}/$_3$ cup blackstrap molasses or
    dark molasses
^{1}/$_4$ cup firmly packed dark brown
    sugar

2 tablespoons apple cider vinegar
1 tablespoon Worcestershire sauce
1 teaspoon dry mustard
^{1}/$_2$ teaspoon salt
^{1}/$_4$ teaspoon freshly ground black
    pepper
3 cups cooked Great Northern
    beans or cannellini (page 170)
3 cups cooked kidney beans
    (page 170)

To prepare the beans: Set a large, heavy pot over medium-high heat and cook the bacon until crisp, about 5 minutes. Transfer the bacon to a plate lined with paper towels to drain, chop the bacon, and set aside.

Discard all but 2 tablespoons of the drippings in the pot. Add the onion, bell pepper, and garlic to the pot and sauté until tender, stirring often, about 8 minutes. Stir in the tomatoes, water, molasses, sugar, vinegar, Worcestershire sauce, mustard, salt, and pepper until the sugar has dissolved. Add the beans and bacon, stirring to combine. Decrease the heat to medium-low and simmer, uncovered, until the mixture begins to thicken, stirring occasionally, about 20 minutes. Taste and correct the seasonings.

Creamy Polenta

6 ounces silken soft tofu, drained

1½ cups rice milk or soy milk

2 teaspoons sugar

¼ teaspoon salt

⅛ teaspoon freshly ground black
   pepper

1 tablespoon pareve margarine

1 cup chicken stock (page 164)

1 cup yellow cornmeal

Chopped parsley for garnish
   (optional)

◎**To prepare the tofu:** In a large bowl, beat the tofu, ¼ cup of the rice milk, sugar, salt, and pepper with an electric mixer until smooth and creamy, about 2 minutes. Set aside.

◎**To prepare the polenta:** Melt the margarine in a large saucepan over medium-low heat, add the chicken stock and remaining 1¼ cups rice milk, and bring to a simmer; do not boil. Decrease the heat to low and gradually add the cornmeal in a slow and steady stream, whisking continuously so that lumps do not form. Whisk the tofu mixture into the cornmeal and continue cooking until the polenta has thickened slightly, 4 to 5 minutes. Garnish with parsley. Serve hot.

Jazz up any meal by spooning this creamy polenta in the center of a plate and topping it with grilled poultry, lamb, fish, or vegetables. It's a snap to prepare and a healthy way to satisfy a craving for something rich and creamy.

Corn Soufflé

Serves 4 to 6

Delicate and flavorful, this soufflé is easy to prepare and makes an elegant addition to grilled chicken or vegetables. The key ingredient—a must for this recipe—is the vanilla rice or soy milk.

3 cups vanilla rice milk or vanilla
   soy milk
1 teaspoon salt
1 cup yellow cornmeal
1/4 cup pareve margarine, cut into
   4 pieces

2 tablespoons sugar
3/4 cup white corn kernels, fresh
   (about 2 ears) or frozen
6 large eggs, separated
1/4 teaspoon cream of tartar

Preheat the oven to 375°. Butter a 2-quart soufflé dish.

To prepare the soufflé: Combine the rice milk and salt in a large saucepan over medium-high and bring to a simmer, taking care not to boil the liquid. Decrease the heat to low. Gradually add the cornmeal in a slow and steady stream, whisking constantly so that lumps do not form, until the mixture begins to thicken, 2 to 3 minutes. Add the margarine and sugar, whisking until the margarine melts and the mixture is smooth, about 1 minute. Stir in the corn. Remove the mixture from the heat and allow to cool slightly, about 10 minutes, stirring occasionally.

Meanwhile, in a large bowl whisk the egg yolks until well blended. Gradually add the cornmeal mixture to the yolks and stir to blend.

Using an electric mixer, beat the egg whites and cream of tartar in a medium bowl at high speed until they form soft peaks. With a rubber spatula, gently fold the whites into the cornmeal mixture until just combined. Do not overmix or the soufflé will not rise. Pour the mixture into the prepared soufflé dish, and bake until the soufflé rises and turns golden brown, 35 to 40 minutes. Serve immediately.

Gingered Carrots

2 tablespoons pareve margarine

1 tablespoon peeled, minced fresh
   ginger

$^1/_3$ cup orange juice

1 tablespoon pure maple syrup

$1^1/_4$ pounds carrots, peeled and cut
   diagonally into $^1/_2$-inch lengths

$^1/_4$ cup coarsely chopped green
   onion, both white and green
   parts

$^1/_4$ teaspoon salt

$^1/_8$ teaspoon freshly ground black
   pepper

To prepare the dish: Melt the margarine in a saucepan over medium-high heat, and sauté the ginger for about 1 minute. Stir in the orange juice and maple syrup, and bring to a boil. Decrease the heat to low and stir in the carrots, coating them with the mixture. Cover and simmer for about 10 minutes. Add the green onion, salt, and pepper, stir to combine, and continue cooking, uncovered, until the glaze thickens slightly and the carrots are tender, about 5 minutes. Taste and correct the seasonings. Serve hot.

These tender glazed carrots have a subtle sweetness with just the right amount of ginger to liven things up. They're so simple to prepare, you can serve them anytime.

Creamed Spinach

This version of a longtime favorite is easy to prepare and is a very satisfying side dish. The creamy-textured sauce can be made ahead of time and reheated slowly before blending in the spinach. Fresh basil, finely julienned and added to the sauce at the last minute, makes a nice addition.

¹/₄ cup pareve margarine
1 large yellow onion, chopped
2 cloves garlic, minced
2¹/₂ pounds fresh spinach,
  stemmed and coarsely chopped
¹/₄ teaspoon salt
¹/₈ teaspoon freshly ground black
  pepper
3 tablespoons flour
³/₄ cup rice milk or soy milk

To prepare the spinach: Melt 2 tablespoons of the margarine in a large sauté pan over medium-high heat. Add the onion and sauté until it is soft but not brown, about 3 minutes. Add the garlic, spinach, salt, and pepper and sauté until the spinach is just wilted, 2 to 3 minutes.

To prepare the sauce: Melt the remaining 2 tablespoons margarine in a saucepan over medium-low heat. Add the flour and cook, whisking constantly, until well blended, about 1 minute. Whisk in the rice milk, half at a time, and cook until the sauce begins to thicken, 4 to 5 minutes, taking care not to boil the sauce. Add the spinach mixture to the sauce, stirring until incorporated and heated through. Taste and correct the seasonings. Serve hot.

Lemon Garlic Crusted Leeks

Serves 4 to 6

6 medium leeks, white and pale
   green parts only
1 large lemon
$^1/_4$ cup pareve margarine
4 cloves garlic, minced

$^1/_3$ cup bread crumbs (page 174)
$^1/_4$ teaspoon salt
$^1/_4$ teaspoon freshly ground black
   pepper

This fabulous trio of leek, lemon, and garlic is a match made in heaven. Crunchy and flavorful, these leeks make a delicious accessory to the main course.

To steam the leeks: Trim the leeks, discarding the dark green leaves. Cut the leeks in half lengthwise and rinse well in cold water, being careful to keep the halves intact. Set aside.

To prepare the lemon and steam the leeks: Using a zester, zest the lemon into a small bowl and set aside. Cut the zested lemon in half, and squeeze 1 teaspoon of juice into the bowl of zest. Squeeze the remaining lemon juice into a large pot equipped with a steaming basket. Add the 2 lemon halves to the pot, along with enough water to steam the leeks. Place the pot over high heat, and bring the water to a boil. Arrange the leeks, cut sides up, in the basket. Fit the basket in the pot, cover, and steam the leeks until slightly tender, 10 to 15 minutes. Drain well. Arrange the leeks, cut sides up, on a buttered baking sheet and set aside. The leeks can be prepared 1 day ahead. If preparing them ahead, cover and refrigerate.

To prepare the topping: Melt the margarine in a saucepan over medium-high heat, and sauté the garlic until tender, 2 to 3 minutes. Remove the saucepan from the heat and add the bread crumbs, lemon zest, salt, and pepper. Stir until blended.

To top and broil the leeks: Preheat the broiler. Place the oven rack 3 to 4 inches from the heat source. Using a teaspoon, spoon the bread crumb mixture onto the cut side of the leeks, and gently pat the mixture down with the back of the spoon. Place the baking sheet under the broiler, and broil until the leeks are golden brown, about 3 minutes. Watch them carefully so they do not burn. Serve hot or warm.

Brussels Sprouts with Shallots and Chestnuts

Brussels sprouts are part of the cabbage family and share many of the same health-enhancing attributes, including an ample amount of antioxidants, vitamins, and minerals. They're ideal for a holiday meal and pair nicely with a wide range of meat dishes. This festive vegetable is simple to make and quick to assemble, especially if you roast the chestnuts in advance.

6 chestnuts
$^1/_2$ teaspoon oil
$1^1/_2$ pounds brussels sprouts, about 4 cups
3 tablespoons pareve margarine
$^1/_2$ pound shallots, thinly sliced
1 to 2 tablespoons pure maple syrup
$^1/_4$ teaspoon salt
$^1/_8$ teaspoon freshly ground black pepper
2 tablespoons minced fresh flat-leaf parsley

To roast the chestnuts: Preheat the oven to 400°. With a small, sharp knife, score the tops of the chestnuts with an X. Place the chestnuts in a small baking dish and rub them with the oil to coat. Roast, uncovered, for about 10 minutes. Remove from the oven and cover the dish with aluminum foil, allowing the chestnuts to steam. Let rest for about 5 minutes. Peel and coarsely chop the chestnuts. You should have about $^1/_3$ cup. Set aside.

To prepare the brussels sprouts: In a large pot fitted with a steaming basket, bring water to a boil over high heat. Trim off the stems of the brussels sprouts, and discard any discolored outer leaves. Cut the brussels sprouts in half lengthwise. Place them in the basket and steam until tender, 8 to 10 minutes. Their color should be bright when you take them from the pot. Rinse under cold running water to stop the cooking, and drain well.

To prepare the shallots and assemble the dish: Melt the margarine in a large sauté pan over medium-high heat. Add the shallots and sauté for about 5 minutes, or until golden. Add the brussels sprouts, chestnuts, maple syrup, salt, and pepper, toss to incorporate, and sauté until heated through, about 2 minutes. Toss with the parsley. Taste and correct the seasonings. Serve hot.

Roasted Vegetable Medley

2 carrots, peeled, halved length-
    wise, and cut into 1-inch pieces

2 red bell peppers, seeded,
    deribbed, and cut into 1-inch
    pieces

2 zucchini, ends trimmed, halved
    lengthwise, and cut into 1-inch
    pieces

2 yellow crookneck squash, ends
    trimmed, halved lengthwise,
    and cut into 1-inch pieces

$1/2$ pound red cabbage, cut into
    1-inch cubes

$1/2$ pound cauliflower, cut into
    florets

2 yellow onions, cut into 1-inch
    pieces

3 tablespoons olive oil

1 tablespoon balsamic vinegar

1 tablespoon minced fresh
    rosemary, or 1 teaspoon dried

2 teaspoons minced fresh thyme,
    or $1/2$ teaspoon dried

2 cloves garlic, minced

$1/2$ teaspoon salt

$1/4$ teaspoon freshly ground black
    pepper

I enjoy serving these vegetables throughout the summer and early fall, when the squash is at its peak. You can use any combination of vegetables, but it's important to cut them to a uniform size so they cook at the same pace. This colorful medley can be served hot with roast meats or as a cold salad.

Preheat the oven to 350°.

To prepare the vegetables: Place the carrots, bell pepper, squash, cabbage, cauliflower, and onion in a large bowl. Whisk the olive oil, vinegar, rosemary, thyme, garlic, salt, and pepper in a small bowl until blended. Pour this mixture over the vegetables and toss thoroughly to coat.

Transfer the vegetables to a shallow roasting pan, and spread them out in a single layer. Roast the vegetables for 20 minutes, turn them with a spatula, and continue roasting until they are tender and brown but not soft, 20 to 30 minutes. Remove the pan from the oven and transfer the vegetables to a bowl to serve.

Pan-Seared Tofu

2 (12-ounce) packages firm or
   extra-firm tofu, drained
1/4 cup soy sauce
1/4 cup orange juice
2 tablespoons dry white wine or
   sake
3 tablespoons olive oil
2 tablespoons minced green onion,
   both white and green parts

2 teaspoons sesame oil
3 cloves garlic, minced
1 teaspoon freshly squeezed lemon
   juice
2 teaspoons peeled, minced fresh
   ginger, or 1 teaspoon ground
1 teaspoon freshly ground black
   pepper

Marinating and then pan-searing tofu gives it both delicious flavor and a satisfying texture that holds up well in sandwiches and makes a great alternative to meat. For this recipe, plan on marinating the tofu for at least 24 hours, allowing it to absorb the flavors completely. Once you've marinated the tofu, use the remaining marinade to make a savory sauce by reducing it in a saucepan. Top Pan-Seared Tofu with Apple Mango Chutney (page 120).

To press the tofu: Place the tofu atop several layers of paper towels on a large plate. Cover the tofu with additional paper towels and then another plate. Place something heavy on top of the plate to weight it down, such as 3 or 4 cans of food. Allow the tofu to drain for about 30 minutes. Replace the wet towels with dry ones and continue to press the tofu for another 30 minutes. Cut the tofu into 1-inch-thick slabs.

To marinate the tofu: Whisk the soy sauce, orange juice, wine, 1 tablespoon of the olive oil, the green onion, sesame oil, garlic, lemon juice, ginger, and pepper in a bowl until blended. Place the drained tofu slabs side by side in a shallow container with a tight-fitting lid. Pour the marinade over the tofu so that the tofu is immersed in the marinade. Cover and refrigerate for 24 to 48 hours.

To sear the tofu: Heat the remaining 2 tablespoons olive oil in a sauté pan over medium-high heat until very hot. Lift the tofu out of the marinade and reserve the marinade for later use. Place the tofu in the hot skillet, partially covering the skillet with a lid to lessen splattering. Sear the tofu until dark brown, about 3 minutes. Turn the tofu over with a spatula and continue to sear the other side for 2 to 3 minutes more. Transfer the tofu to a plate.

To make the sauce: Pour the marinade into the hot skillet. Whisking constantly, bring the marinade to a boil. Decrease the heat to medium-low, and reduce the marinade by one-third. Serve the tofu with a small amount of sauce spooned on top.

Broiled Polenta with Vegetable Ragout

Colorful and full of flavor, this dish is wonderful served alongside grilled chicken or fish. Accompanied by a salad, it makes a perfect light entrée. Sweet summer vegetables including eggplant, red pepper, and zucchini are sautéed with onion, garlic, and basil—a delightful complement to the polenta.

Polenta

4$^1/_2$ cups rice milk or soy milk

1 teaspoon salt

2 cups yellow cornmeal

......

Ragout

$^1/_4$ cup olive oil

1 large yellow onion, halved and
   thinly sliced

2 Japanese eggplants, or 1 small
   globe eggplant, cut into
   $^1/_2$-inch cubes

3 cloves garlic, minced

2 teaspoons salt

1 red bell pepper, seeded, deribbed,
   and chopped into $^1/_2$-inch
   pieces

2 zucchini, halved lengthwise and
   sliced $^1/_4$-inch thick

2 cups chopped tomatoes
   (page 166)

$^1/_3$ cup hand-torn fresh basil leaves

1 teaspoon sugar

$^1/_2$ teaspoon freshly ground black
   pepper

......

Basil sprigs for garnish (optional)

To prepare the polenta: Combine the rice milk and salt in a large saucepan over medium-high heat, and bring a simmer; do not boil. Decrease the heat to low, and gradually add the cornmeal in a slow and steady stream, whisking constantly so that lumps do not form. Continue whisking until the mixture is thick and pulls away from the side of the pan, about 10 minutes. Pour the polenta into a nonstick 8-inch loaf pan. Using a rubber spatula, smooth the top out evenly, and allow the mixture to cool for about 45 minutes. Cover the pan with plastic wrap, and refrigerate for 1 hour or overnight.

To prepare the ragout: Heat 2 tablespoons of the olive oil in a large skillet over medium-high heat, add the onion, and sauté for about 3 minutes. Add the eggplant, garlic, and salt, and sauté stirring often, for 5 to 6 minutes. Add the bell pepper, zucchini, tomatoes, basil, sugar, and pepper, and sauté for about 3 minutes. Cover and simmer the vegetables over low heat, stirring occasionally, for about 5 minutes. Remove the skillet from the heat and set aside. Taste and correct the seasonings.

◢ **To grill and assemble the dish:** Preheat the grill or broiler. Turn the polenta out onto a cutting board, and slice it into sixteen $^1/_2$-inch-thick pieces. Next, slice each piece diagonally, forming 2 triangles, or create various shapes such as leaves, half moons, and circles by using large cookie cutters. Place the cut pieces of polenta on a cookie sheet and, using a pastry brush, brush both sides generously with the remaining 2 tablespoons olive oil. Broil or grill each side for 1 to 3 minutes, or until lightly browned. Transfer to serving plates. To serve as a starter or side dish, arrange 2 slices of the grilled polenta on a plate and spoon the ragout on top, garnishing with basil sprigs. As an entrée, arrange 4 slices per plate.

Apple–Corn Bread Stuffing

Makes about
10 cups

Corn Bread

1¹/₂ cups yellow cornmeal

1¹/₂ cups flour

6 tablespoons sugar

1 tablespoon baking powder

¹/₂ teaspoon baking soda

1 teaspoon salt

1¹/₂ cups rice milk or soy milk

2 large eggs

¹/₂ cup corn oil

......

Stuffing

8 slices turkey bacon or pork
   bacon

1 tablespoon olive oil

1 large yellow onion, finely
   chopped

1 cup chopped celery (about
   3 stalks)

3 cups cubed French bread, crusts
   removed and lightly toasted

2 large apples, Pippin or Golden
   Delicious, cored, peeled, and
   cut into ¹/₂-inch pieces

³/₄ cup pine nuts, toasted
   (page 175)

²/₃ cup golden raisins or dark
   raisins

¹/₄ cup chopped fresh flat-leaf
   parsley

3 tablespoons chopped fresh sage,
   or 1 tablespoon dried

2 tablespoons minced fresh thyme,
   or 2 teaspoons dried

1 teaspoon salt

¹/₂ teaspoon freshly ground black
   pepper

3 large eggs

3 cups chicken stock (page 164)

Moist and savory, this corn bread stuffing is a Thanksgiving classic. It can be made in three stages, making the final assembly a snap. It also makes more stuffing then the bird can accommodate, so you will need to bake the extra separately. Plan on mixing the two stuffings together before serving; the stuffing from the bird will have collected all of the wonderful juices, and the stuffing from the dish will provide a slightly crunchy texture.

Preheat the oven to 400°.

To make the corn bread: Oil an 8 by 11 by 2-inch baking dish. Set aside. Combine the cornmeal, flour, sugar, baking powder, baking soda, and salt in a large bowl. Mix together with a whisk until blended. Whisk together the rice milk, eggs, and oil in a small bowl. Pour the egg mixture into the cornmeal mixture, and stir with a large spoon until just combined. Pour the batter into the prepared baking dish. Bake until the top is golden brown and a toothpick inserted in the center comes out clean, 25 to 30 minutes. Remove the corn bread from the oven, and allow it to cool in the dish for about 1 hour.

When the corn bread is cool, preheat the oven to 325°. Cut the corn bread into ¹/₂-inch cubes. Scatter the cubes onto 2 baking sheets, and toast until they are dry but not hard, about 20 minutes. Cool completely on the baking sheets. The bread cubes can be made 2 to 3 days ahead and stored at room temperature in tightly sealed plastic bags.

To prepare the stuffing: Preheat the oven to 325°. Oil an 8 by 8 by 2-inch baking dish. Set aside. Cook the bacon in a skillet over medium-high heat until crisp. Transfer to paper towels to drain. Once the bacon has cooled, crumble into pieces and set aside. Add the oil to the same skillet. When hot, add the onion and celery and sauté until softened, about 6 minutes.

In an extra-large bowl, combine the corn bread cubes, crumbled bacon, onion mixture, French bread, apples, pine nuts, raisins, parsley, sage, thyme, salt, and pepper; toss to mix. The stuffing can be made to this point 1 day ahead if covered tightly and refrigerated.

Just before using the stuffing: Whisk together the eggs and 2 cups of the chicken stock in a small bowl. Pour the egg mixture over the corn bread mixture and toss together until the corn bread mixture is thoroughly moistened but not mushy. Loosely fill the main and neck cavities of the turkey with the stuffing. Pour the remaining 1 cup stock over the remaining stuffing, and toss to mix. Spoon the stuffing into the prepared baking dish, cover with aluminum foil, and bake for 1 hour. Uncover the dish and bake until the top begins to crisp, about 10 minutes more.

Sauces, Relishes, Butters, and Rubs

When cooking dairy-free, it's important to use flavor enhancers—well-chosen sauces, condiments, spice mixtures, and so on that make a simple dish sparkle. This chapter offers a number of recipes that will give your meals a flavor boost without the use of dairy products. The butters marry beautifully with vegetables, breads, and egg dishes; the rubs add a new dimension to grilled meats, fish, and tofu. There's a creamy hollandaise to enjoy with eggs, a relish to complement the Thanksgiving turkey, and a zesty peanut sauce to toss with pasta. These sauces, relishes, butters, and rubs are modest by themselves, but they have the ability to transform and complete other foods, and the best part is, they're all dairy-free!

Hollandaise Sauce

1/2 cup pareve margarine
3 large egg yolks, at room
temperature
1 tablespoon freshly squeezed
lemon juice

Pinch of cayenne pepper
1 tablespoon dry vermouth or dry
white wine

Heavenly and rich, hollandaise sauce is a must for Eggs Florentine (page 18) and a decadent addition to roast beef or vegetables. This sauce can be a little tricky to make; just remember not to let the mixture overheat, or the sauce will break.

To prepare the sauce: Melt the margarine in a small saucepan over low heat. When it is completely melted, remove from the heat and keep warm.

Place the egg yolks, lemon juice, and cayenne in the top of a double boiler over just simmering, not boiling, water. The bottom of the upper pan should not touch the simmering water in the lower pan. Whisk the mixture until it thickens and forms a sheen, 3 to 5 minutes. Whisking constantly, add the margarine, a few drops in the beginning, then increasing to a slow and steady stream, until all of the margarine has been added. Add the vermouth, whisking until incorporated and the sauce is light and fluffy. Remove the sauce from the heat and serve immediately.

Béchamel Sauce

1/4 cup pareve margarine
1/3 cup flour
1 1/2 cups warm rice milk or soy milk

1/8 teaspoon ground nutmeg
1/4 teaspoon salt
1/8 teaspoon ground white pepper

The classic white sauce, béchamel is used as the basis for a wide variety of "creamed" dishes. It is the starting point for many casseroles, such as the Wild Mushroom Lasagna (page 80).

To prepare the sauce: Melt the margarine in a large saucepan over low heat. Whisking constantly, add the flour and cook until it is incorporated and the roux is bubbling, about 1 minute. Increase the heat to medium-low and whisk in the rice milk, 1/2 cup at a time, until a smooth sauce develops and thickens, 8 to 10 minutes. Take care not to boil the sauce. Whisk in the nutmeg, salt, and pepper. Taste and correct the seasonings. Serve warm.

Pepper Bean Sauce

Makes 4 cups

1 tablespoon olive oil

1 large yellow onion, chopped

3 cloves garlic, minced

2 cups chicken stock (page 164)

1 large red bell pepper, roasted
(page 169) and cut into
quarters

2 cups garbanzo beans, cooked
and drained (page 170)

$^1/_4$ cup dry white wine

$1^1/_2$ tablespoons yellow curry
powder

$^1/_8$ teaspoon crushed red pepper
flakes

$^1/_4$ teaspoon salt

1 teaspoon seasoned rice vinegar

To prepare the sauce: Heat the olive oil in a large sauté pan over medium-high heat, and sauté the onion until tender, about 3 minutes. Add the garlic and sauté for about 1 minute. Stir in the chicken stock, roasted pepper, beans, wine, curry powder, red pepper flakes, and salt. Bring to a boil, decrease the heat to low, and simmer until the beans break apart easily with a fork, 25 to 30 minutes. Ladle the ingredients into a blender, cover tightly, and purée until smooth, about 2 minutes. Transfer the sauce back to the saucepan, stir in the rice vinegar, and warm over low heat, stirring occasionally, until the sauce is heated through. Taste and correct the seasonings. Serve warm.

Spicy or mild, this bean sauce is a colorful addition to the Curry Vegetable Wontons (page 31) or grilled fish or chicken. It can be made up to 1 day ahead and stored in a covered nonmetallic container in the refrigerator.

Black Bean Sauce

Makes 3 cups

This rich and robust sauce has a touch of lime juice, which adds a delicate piquant flavor to the beans. To use the sauce as a delicious dip for tortilla chips, simply decrease the cooking liquid to $^1/_2$ cup when puréeing the mixture, and don't bother to warm it up. Canned beans are not suitable for this recipe, since both the flavor and the color of the sauce would be compromised.

2 cups cooked black beans
(page 170)
1 cup reserved black bean cooking
liquid
$^1/_2$ cup finely chopped yellow
onion
3 cloves garlic, minced
1 jalapeño pepper, seeded and
minced, more or less to taste

3 tablespoons freshly squeezed lime
juice
$^1/_2$ teaspoon ground cumin
$^1/_2$ teaspoon salt
$^1/_8$ teaspoon freshly ground black
pepper

To prepare the sauce: Combine the beans, reserved liquid, onion, garlic, jalapeño, lime juice, cumin, salt, and pepper in a blender. Cover tightly and purée for 1 minute. The sauce will appear smooth, with dark flecks throughout. Transfer the puréed mixture to a saucepan. Set the saucepan over medium-low heat and stir occasionally until the sauce is heated through, about 8 minutes. Take care not to boil the sauce. Taste and correct the seasonings. Serve warm or at room temperature.

Sundried Tomato Cream

Makes 1¹/₂ cups

1 cup dry white wine

¹/₄ cup white wine vinegar

1¹/₂ tablespoons freshly squeezed
    lemon juice (about 1 lemon)

8 whole black peppercorns

4 sprigs flat-leaf parsley

2 sprigs thyme

¹/₄ cup chopped celery leaves

1 bay leaf

¹/₄ cup oil-packed sundried
    tomatoes

6 ounces silken soft tofu

¹/₄ cup rice milk or soy milk

1 clove garlic, minced

2 tablespoons chopped fresh
    flat-leaf parsley

Salt

Freshly ground black pepper

To prepare the sauce: Combine the wine, vinegar, lemon juice, pepper-corns, parsley and thyme sprigs, celery leaves, and bay leaf in a small saucepan over high heat. Boil the liquid until it is reduced to ¹/₄ cup, about 10 minutes. Strain the liquid through a fine sieve into a small bowl, and discard the solids left in the sieve.

Place the sundried tomatoes, tofu, rice milk, garlic, parsley, and wine mixture in a blender. Purée the mixture at top speed, scraping down the sides of the blender with a spatula, until smooth, about 1 minute. Return the mixture to the same saucepan, and simmer over medium-low heat, stirring occasionally, for about 3 minutes to allow the flavors to fully blend. Taste and correct the seasonings with salt and freshly ground black pepper. Serve warm.

This brilliant sauce makes a zesty addition to grilled chicken or fish. Add a tablespoon to grain dishes, such as the Creamy Polenta (page 99), or spoon it over Eggs Florentine (page 18) in place of the hollandaise sauce for a bright and flavorful finish.

Spicy Peanut Sauce

This lively sauce combines rich sesame oil and honey with minced ginger, giving it a refreshing finish. Select a creamy-style peanut butter for this recipe, with little or no added sugar or salt. If you are using an old-fashioned peanut butter, the type where the oil rises to the surface, be sure to mix the oil back in thoroughly before adding it to this recipe, or the sauce will separate once it cools.

1 cup smooth peanut butter

$^1/_2$ cup boiling water (add more in small increments if needed)

3 tablespoons sesame oil

3 tablespoons honey

2 tablespoons soy sauce

2 tablespoons rice vinegar

3 cloves garlic, minced

1 tablespoon peeled, minced fresh ginger

$^1/_8$ teaspoon crushed red pepper flakes

To prepare the sauce: Combine the peanut butter and water in a bowl and stir until smooth. Add the sesame oil, honey, soy sauce, vinegar, garlic, ginger, and pepper flakes. Stir until well blended and smooth. To thin or rewarm the sauce, slowly stir in boiling water, a little at a time, until the desired consistency is achieved. Do not reheat it in a saucepan or in the microwave, or the sauce will break. Serve at room temperature.

Note: If you will be using this sauce with the Asian Peanut Pasta Salad (page 40) and need to adapt this recipe into a vegan one, simply omit the honey and replace it with $1^1/_2$ tablespoons of sugar. Stir the sugar, peanut butter, and boiling water together until smooth, and then add the other ingredients.

Mustard Cream Sauce

Makes 1¹/₄ cups

3/4 cup lager beer

2 tablespoons minced green onion, both white and green parts

2 tablespoons pareve margarine

2 tablespoons flour

2/3 cup chicken stock (page 164), more if needed

1 tablespoon chopped fresh tarragon, or 1 teaspoon dried

1¹/2 tablespoons tarragon white wine vinegar or white wine vinegar

1/4 cup Dijon mustard

2 teaspoons whole mustard seeds

1 tablespoon honey

Brush this tangy, sweet sauce liberally onto pork, lamb, or chicken before grilling, or spoon it over cooked meats or grilled tofu.

To prepare the sauce: Combine the beer and green onion in a small saucepan over high heat. Boil until the liquid is reduced to ¹/4 cup, about 10 minutes. Meanwhile, melt the margarine in a saucepan over low heat. Whisking constantly, add the flour and cook until it is incorporated and the roux is bubbling, about 1 minute. Slowly whisk in the chicken stock, tarragon, vinegar, mustard, mustard seeds, honey, and beer mixture, and simmer for about 3 minutes to allow the flavors to fully blend. Serve hot.

Mushroom Sauce

Makes 2¹/2 cups

3 tablespoons pareve margarine

1/4 cup flour

1 cup warm rice milk or soy milk

3/4 pound fresh button mushrooms, thinly sliced

1 tablespoon cream sherry

1/4 teaspoon salt

1/8 teaspoon ground white pepper

Slightly sweet with a velvety texture, this sauce is lovely served over Sweet Basil Turkey Loaf (page 72), Garlic Mashed Potatoes (page 93), or grilled pork chops.

To prepare the sauce: Melt the margarine in a large saucepan over low heat. Whisking constantly, add the flour until it is incorporated and the roux is bubbling, about 1 minute. Whisk in the rice milk, ¹/2 cup at a time, until a smooth sauce develops and thickens, about 5 minutes, taking care not to boil the sauce. Blend in the mushrooms, cover, and continue simmering, stirring occasionally, until the mixture is reduced by half, 6 to 7 minutes. Remove the saucepan from the heat and stir in the sherry, salt, and pepper. Serve hot.

Creamy Giblet Gravy

Turkey and mashed pota-
toes with homemade
giblet gravy—just the
thought of it makes my
mouth water. To help keep
the last-minute steps to a
minimum, I recommend
preparing the turkey stock
and giblets the day before;
then you'll have time to
prepare the gravy while the
turkey is resting.

Reserved turkey neck, heart, and
   gizzard
4 cups water
5$^{1}/_{2}$ cups chicken stock (page 164)
$^{1}/_{2}$ cup dry vermouth or white
   wine
2 carrots, peeled and coarsely
   chopped
1 large yellow onion, halved

2 large stalks celery, coarsely
   chopped
1 bay leaf
Pan juices from Herb-Roasted
   Turkey (page 88)
5 tablespoons pareve margarine
$^{1}/_{2}$ cup flour
$^{1}/_{4}$ cup rice milk or soy milk

To prepare the stock: Combine the turkey neck, heart, gizzard, water, chicken stock, vermouth, carrots, onion, celery, and bay leaf in a large stockpot over high heat. Bring to a rapid boil and skim off any foam that rises to the top. Decrease the heat to medium, and simmer, uncovered, until stock is reduced to 3 cups, about 2 hours. Remove the pot from the heat and strain the stock into a large nonmetallic bowl. Reserve the turkey neck and giblets. Remove the meat from the turkey neck, and mince the neck meat and the giblets. Set the stock and minced meat aside, or cover and refrigerate overnight.

To prepare the gravy: Pour the turkey pan juices into a large glass bowl. Spoon off any fat that rises to the surface, and discard. Return the pan juices to the roasting pan. Position the roasting pan over 2 burners, set on medium-high heat. Simmer the pan juices for 2 to 3 minutes, and deglaze the pan by scraping any loose particles from the bottom and sides with a wooden spoon. Remove the pan from the heat, and strain into a bowl.

Melt the margarine in a large saucepan over medium-low heat. Whisking constantly, add the flour and cook until it is incorporated and the roux is bubbling, about 1 minute. Gradually whisk in the turkey stock, 1 cup at a time, until blended. Add the turkey pan juices and simmer, whisking occasionally, until the gravy thickens, about 8 minutes. Whisk in the rice milk and the chopped neck and giblet meat. Taste and correct the seasonings. Serve hot.

Orange Cranberry Relish

1¹/₄ cups sugar

2 tablespoons frozen orange juice
    concentrate, thawed

1 (12-ounce) package fresh
    cranberries

1 tablespoon grated orange zest
    (about 1 orange)

2 tablespoons Triple Sec or Grand
    Marnier

1¹/₂ cups fresh mandarin orange
    segments, peeled, seeded, and
    halved

To prepare and bake the relish: Preheat the oven to 325°. Combine the sugar and orange juice concentrate in an 8 by 8 by 2-inch baking dish, and stir to blend. Add the cranberries to the orange juice mixture and toss to coat. Cover the dish with aluminum foil and bake until the cranberries are very soft and the mixture is juicy, about 50 minutes. Uncover the dish and, with the back of a fork, mash the cranberries to the desired consistency or, if you prefer leave them whole. With a spoon, stir in the orange zest, liqueur, and mandarin oranges until blended. Return the dish to the oven and continue baking, uncovered, for an additional 20 minutes. Remove from the oven and cool completely, about 1¹/₂ hours. The sauce will thicken as it cools, about 1¹/₂ hours. Cover and refrigerate for 4 hours or overnight. Serve at room temperature.

I began making this cranberry relish for my family several years ago, and it quickly became a staple at our Thanksgiving table. It is incredibly simple to prepare, and making it 2 or 3 days in advance gives the flavors a chance to fully blend. Serve it at room temperature.

Apple Mango Chutney

Spicy or mild, this chutney jazzes up the simplest of meals. Serve it alongside the Pan-Seared Tofu (page 106) or with grilled pork or chicken. Keep in mind that the heat of the crushed red pepper flakes will intensify as the mixture simmers; a pinch goes a long way. This chutney improves with time and will keep, covered in the refrigerator, for up to 1 week.

1³/4 pounds Pippin apples, peeled, cored, and minced

1 ripe mango, peeled, pitted, and cut into 1/2-inch pieces

1 large yellow onion, finely chopped

¹/3 cup golden raisins

¹/4 cup red wine vinegar

¹/2 teaspoon freshly squeezed lemon juice

2 tablespoons firmly packed dark brown sugar

2 tablespoons granulated sugar

1 tablespoon peeled, minced fresh ginger, or 1 teaspoon ground

¹/2 teaspoon ground turmeric

¹/8 teaspoon salt

Pinch of crushed red pepper flakes

To prepare the chutney: Combine the apples, mango, onion, raisins, vinegar, lemon juice, sugars, ginger, turmeric, salt, and pepper flakes in a large saucepan over medium-high heat, and stir to blend. Bring to a boil. Cover the saucepan, cracking the lid to allow steam to escape, decrease the heat to low, and simmer for about 1 hour, stirring occasionally. Remove the saucepan from the heat and allow the mixture to cool for about 2 hours. Transfer the chutney to a container with a tight-fitting lid and refrigerate. Before serving, stir the chutney and allow it to reach room temperature.

Pico de Gallo

Makes 1 1/2 cups

1 pound ripe tomatoes, seeded and
    diced

1/2 cup finely chopped red onion
    (about 1/2 small onion)

1/3 cup finely chopped fresh
    cilantro

2 tablespoons freshly squeezed lime
    juice (about 2 limes)

1 jalapeño pepper, seeded and
    minced, more or less to taste

1/4 teaspoon salt

1/8 teaspoon freshly ground black
    pepper

To prepare the salsa: Combine the tomato, onion, cilantro, lime juice, jalapeño, salt, and pepper in a nonmetallic bowl, and toss to combine. Taste and correct the seasonings. Serve immediately, or cover the bowl tightly and refrigerate for up to 2 days. Just before serving, gently toss the salsa to mix. Serve chilled or at room temperature.

This traditional salsa recipe comes from Gerard Rodriguez, a gifted chef who I have had the pleasure of working with. It has been in his family for generations. If sweet yellow tomatoes are available, combine them with the red tomatoes for a brilliant burst of color.

Kiwi Papaya Salsa

Makes 3 cups

1 cup peeled, diced kiwi, in
    1/4-inch pieces (3 to 4 kiwi)

1 1/2 cups peeled, seeded, and diced
    ripe papaya, in 1/4-inch pieces
    (about 1 large papaya)

1/3 cup minced chives (2 to 3
    bunches)

2 ripe plum tomatoes, seeded and
    diced

2 teaspoons freshly squeezed lime
    juice

1 teaspoon grated lime zest

1/4 teaspoon salt

1/8 teaspoon freshly ground black
    pepper

1/3 cup finely chopped fresh
    flat-leaf parsley

To prepare the salsa: Combine the kiwi, papaya, chives, tomato, lime juice, zest, salt, and pepper in a nonmetallic bowl, and toss together. Cover the bowl tightly and refrigerate for up to 2 hours. Just before serving, add the parsley and toss gently to mix. Taste and correct the seasonings. Serve chilled.

Fresh, bright, and colorful, this salsa is delicious with Salmon Cakes (page 26) and works equally well atop grilled fish or chicken. Try serving it as a dip with white or blue corn chips instead of regular salsa.

Applesauce

Applesauce was one of the first dishes I learned to cook as a youngster, and cook it I did. My poor family endured more applesauce than anyone could imagine, eating it for breakfast, lunch, and dinner. Just when they thought they were out of the woods, I would concoct a new flavor by adding cinnamon or fresh berries. Recently, when I told my mom that I would be adding a recipe for applesauce to my book, she laughed and said it would be the best recipe ever.

$1^1/_2$ pounds Granny Smith or Pippin apples, peeled, cored, and sliced

$1^1/_2$ pounds Gala or McIntosh apples, peeled, cored, and sliced

$^1/_2$ cup water

1 tablespoon sugar, or to taste

1 tablespoon freshly squeezed lemon juice, or to taste

To prepare the applesauce: Combine the apples and water in a large saucepan over medium-low heat. Cover and cook until the apples are very soft, about 20 minutes, stirring occasionally. Transfer the apples to a bowl and mash with a fork or potato masher. Taste the sauce and add sugar and lemon juice to taste, depending on the flavor of the apples. Serve warm or at room temperature. To store the sauce, cover and refrigerate.

Note: Any type of apples can be used to make applesauce; however, I prefer a combination of varieties, and I enjoy leaving them slightly chunky. If you prefer a smooth sauce, pass the cooked apples through a food mill.

Lean Sour Cream

Makes 1³/₄ cups

1 (12-ounce) package silken soft
    tofu, drained
¹/₄ cup rice milk or soy milk
1 tablespoon freshly squeezed
    lemon juice

1 tablespoon white wine vinegar
¹/₄ teaspoon salt

To prepare the sour cream: Place the tofu, rice milk, lemon juice, vinegar, and salt in a blender with a lid. Purée the mixture at top speed, scraping down the sides of the blender with a spatula, until smooth, about 1 minute. Transfer the mixture to a container with a tight-fitting lid. The sour cream will keep, covered and refrigerated, for 2 days. Serve chilled, stirring with a spoon before serving.

Even though sour cream may no longer be a part of my diet, I still want it on my baked potato. This soy version satisfies my craving and has all the flavor—without all the fat—of conventional dairy sour cream.

Sorrel Herb Butter

Makes about
¹/₃ cup

1 bunch sorrel
¹/₄ cup pareve margarine, at room
    temperature
1 tablespoon finely chopped chives
    (about ¹/₂ bunch)
1 teaspoon grated lemon zest

To prepare the butter: Clean the sorrel by rinsing, patting dry with paper towels, and removing the center stem. The center stem can be removed by folding the leaf in half lengthwise and cut or pull the stem off, as if cleaning snap peas. Discard the stems and finely chop the leaves. Place the margarine, chives, zest, and sorrel in a small bowl, and cream the mixture together until well blended. Cover and refrigerate. Serve chilled.

This butter is simple to make and enhances the flavor of many foods. Try adding a spoonful to scrambled eggs or to Yukon Gold Potato-Leek Soup (page 49) to add a new dimension to the dish.

Creole Butter

Makes about
$^1/_3$ cup

This colorful, spicy butter adds a taste of New Orleans served atop a piece of grilled fish or chicken. It is also excellent stirred into rice or beans, when a spicy lift is desired. If you like it hot, add more cayenne pepper.

$^1/_4$ cup pareve margarine, at room
    temperature
2 cloves garlic, minced
1 teaspoon paprika
1 shallot, finely chopped

$^1/_4$ teaspoon Worcestershire sauce
$^1/_4$ teaspoon coarsely ground black
    pepper
$^1/_8$ teaspoon cayenne pepper

To prepare the butter: Place the margarine, garlic, paprika, shallot, Worcestershire sauce, pepper, and cayenne in a small bowl, and cream the mixture together until well blended. Cover and refrigerate. Serve chilled.

Mustard Tarragon Butter

Makes about
$^1/_3$ cup

This lively butter goes especially well with many calcium-rich vegetables, such as kale, collard greens, bok choy, and cabbage. Tarragon is best used fresh—its sweet fragrance lightens the taste of whatever it is paired with.

$^1/_4$ cup pareve margarine, at room
    temperature
1 teaspoon grated lemon zest
$^1/_4$ teaspoon freshly squeezed
    lemon juice
2 teaspoons Dijon mustard

2 tablespoons finely chopped fresh
    tarragon
1 shallot, finely chopped
$^1/_8$ teaspoon freshly ground black
    pepper

To prepare the butter: Place the margarine, zest, lemon juice, mustard, tarragon, shallot, and pepper, in a small bowl, and cream the mixture together until well blended. Cover and refrigerate. Serve chilled.

Orange Honey Butter ✳

^{1}/$_3$ cup pareve margarine, at room
    temperature
1 tablespoon minced orange zest
    (about 1 orange)
1 tablespoon honey

⌇**To prepare the butter:** Place the margarine, zest, and honey in a small bowl, and cream the mixture together until well blended. Cover and refrigerate. Serve chilled.

Makes about
^{1}/$_3$ cup

Simplicity never tasted so good. Spread this butter on a warm piece of Sweet Potato Corn Bread (page 136) or on Orange Cornmeal Popovers (page 133), or use it in place of maple syrup on French toast.

Southern Spicy Rub

3 tablespoons firmly packed dark
    brown sugar
2 tablespoons coarsely ground
    black pepper
2 tablespoons paprika

1 tablespoon garlic powder
1 tablespoon onion powder
1 tablespoon coarse salt
^{1}/$_4$ teaspoon cayenne pepper

⌇**To prepare the rub:** Place the brown sugar, pepper, paprika, garlic powder, onion powder, salt, and cayenne in a small bowl, and mix to blend. Store the rub in a tightly covered container in a cool, dry place. It is best if used within a couple months. When ready to use, first pat the uncooked chicken, fish, meat, or tofu dry with paper towels, then coat well with the rub.

Makes about
^{3}/$_4$ cup

Hot and zesty, this rub is great with grilled food; it can be used on chicken, meat, firm white fish such as halibut, scallops, prawns, and tofu. If you want to turn up the heat, try adding up to 1 teaspoon of cayenne pepper.

Mediterranean Rub

This basic rub has been a staple in our family for generations. It started with my Baba (grandmother) who roasted the most succulent chickens, Cornish game hens, and turkey you could imagine. Now I prepare roast chicken and vegetables using this rub at least once a week. While it is cooking, I simply sit back and enjoy the aroma of rosemary and herbs as they fill the kitchen.

¹/₄ cup minced fresh rosemary
2 tablespoons olive oil
1 tablespoon minced fresh oregano
1 tablespoon minced fresh thyme

2 teaspoons garlic powder
1 teaspoon coarse salt
¹/₂ teaspoon coarsely ground black
  pepper

To prepare the rub: Place the rosemary, olive oil, oregano, thyme, garlic, salt, and pepper in a small bowl and mix to blend. Rub onto poultry, meat, or vegetables before cooking. Store any unused rub in a covered container, and refrigerate for up to 1 week.

Quick Breads

My father has always loved bread and, in fact, made his living working for a bakery. When I was a child, he would take me for rides in his bread truck—the intoxicating aroma of the freshly baked bread along with the treasured moments shared with my dad made my heart soar. Like my father, I have a love of bread, my specialty being quick breads. From breakfast Cinnamon Rolls (page 128) and Golden Maple Raisin Scones (page 129) to Green Onion–Rosemary Drop Biscuits (page 135) and Orange Cornmeal Popovers (page 133), quick breads are just what the name implies: easy to prepare and very satisfying. For flawless results when making quick bread doughs or batters, I apply a simple rule of thumb: the less you handle them, the more tender and delicate the outcome.

Cinnamon Rolls

Waking up to the smell of
freshly baked cinnamon
rolls is a wonderful way to
start any morning. These
rolls are smaller than their
commercial cousins but
just as satisfying. They
have a biscuitlike quality
and are at their best warm
from the oven.

¹/₄ cup granulated sugar
2 tablespoons firmly packed light
*   brown sugar*
1 tablespoon ground cinnamon
3 cups flour
4 teaspoons baking powder

¹/₂ teaspoon salt
¹/₂ cup pareve margarine
1 cup rice milk or soy milk
¹/₄ cup finely chopped pecans
¹/₄ cup golden raisins

Preheat the oven to 425°. Lightly grease a cookie sheet with a small amount of pareve margarine.

In a small bowl, combine the sugars and cinnamon; set aside.

To prepare the dough: Combine the flour, baking powder, and salt in a large bowl. Mix together with a whisk until blended. Add 6 tablespoons of the margarine, and crumble the mixture through your fingers until it resembles coarse sand. Add the rice milk and quickly work the dough into a ball with your hands. Do not overwork the dough or it will become tough.

To roll out the dough: Place the dough on a lightly floured work surface. Using a rolling pin, roll the dough into a 12 by 18-inch rectangle, ¹/₄ inch thick, dusting with additional flour as needed. With a sharp knife, trim off any excess dough. Position the dough so that you are facing one of the long 18-inch sides. Using a rubber spatula, spread the remaining 2 tablespoons of softened margarine evenly over the dough. Sprinkle the dough with the cinnamon sugar, pecans, and raisins, leaving a ¹/₂-inch border on the wide side farthest from you.

To form the rolls: Beginning with the wide side closest to you, roll the dough up tightly to form one 18-inch log. Seal it by pinching the edges of the dough together. Cut the roll into 1¹/₂-inch slices. Place the slices cut side down on the prepared baking sheet. Bake for 15 minutes, or until golden brown. Remove from the oven and loosen the rolls from the bottom of the baking sheet. Allow them to cool slightly before serving.

Golden Maple Raisin Scones

$^1/_2$ cup pure maple syrup

$^1/_2$ cup rice milk or soy milk

1 cup golden raisins

3 cups flour

5 tablespoons firmly packed light
   brown sugar

$1^1/_2$ teaspoons baking powder

$^1/_2$ teaspoon baking soda

$^1/_2$ cup pareve margarine, cut into
   $^1/_2$-inch pieces

1 egg, beaten

Preheat the oven to 375°.

To prepare the dough: Whisk together the syrup and rice milk in a small bowl. Stir in the raisins and set aside.

Combine the flour, 3 tablespoons of the brown sugar, baking powder, and baking soda in a large bowl and mix together with a whisk. Add the margarine and crumble the mixture through your fingertips until it resembles coarse pebbles. Slowly add the liquid to the flour mixture and stir until the dough starts to come together. Turn the dough out onto a lightly floured surface. Gently knead the dough for 5 or 6 turns, adding more flour if necessary and being careful not to overwork the dough.

To form and bake the scones: Pat the dough out to form an 8-inch round. Using a pastry brush, lightly coat the round with the egg and sprinkle with the remaining 2 tablespoons brown sugar. Cut the round evenly into 8 wedges. Transfer the wedges to an ungreased insulated baking sheet, placing them about 2 inches apart.

Bake the scones until the tops are golden brown or until a tester inserted into the center of a scone comes out clean, about 20 minutes. Serve warm, or allow to cool completely on a wire rack, about 35 minutes, before storing in an airtight container.

My husband loves these scones warm out of the oven: They have a fine, tender crumb and a rich yet delicate maple flavor. The secret to having a tender crumb is in working the chilled margarine into the flour; once incorporated, the pieces of margarine should be the size of peas. These scones are amazingly easy to make and are a special addition to breakfast, brunch, or high tea.

Lemon Poppyseed Muffins

These fragrant muffins have a tart, refreshing taste of lemon, complemented by a delightful light crunch from the poppyseeds. Ginger lovers can easily adapt this recipe to make Lemon Ginger Muffins by substituting 3 tablespoons of peeled, grated fresh ginger for the poppyseeds.

2 cups flour
1 tablespoon baking powder
1/2 teaspoon baking soda
1/4 teaspoon salt
1/2 cup sugar
2 tablespoons poppyseeds
2 large eggs

1 cup rice milk or soy milk
1 tablespoon freshly squeezed
    lemon juice
1/4 cup pareve margarine, melted
    and cooled
2 tablespoons chopped lemon zest
    (from 3 to 4 lemons)

Position the rack in the center of the oven and preheat the oven to 400°. Coat a muffin pan with cooking spray, and set aside.

To prepare the batter: Combine the flour, baking powder, baking soda, salt, sugar, and poppyseeds in a large bowl. Mix together with a whisk until blended. Whisk together the eggs, rice milk, lemon juice, margarine, and zest in a small bowl until well blended. Stir the egg mixture into the flour mixture until just combined, taking care not to overmix the batter. The batter should look lumpy.

To bake the muffins: Spoon the batter into the prepared muffin tins, filling each cup two-thirds full. Any cups that are not filled with batter should be filled halfway with water to allow for even baking. Bake the muffins until golden brown and a tester inserted in the middle comes out clean, about 20 minutes. Remove the pan from the oven and let cool for about 10 minutes. Transfer the muffins to a wire rack and cool completely.

Blueberry Oat Bran Muffins

1 1/4 cups all-purpose flour

3/4 cup whole-wheat flour

1 tablespoon baking powder

1 teaspoon baking soda

1/4 teaspoon salt

1/3 cup wheat or oat bran

1/3 cup quick oats

1/3 cup wheat germ

3/4 cup firmly packed light brown sugar

2 large eggs

1 cup vanilla rice milk or vanilla soy milk

1/4 cup pareve margarine, melted and cooled

1 tablespoon freshly squeezed lemon juice

1 cup fresh blueberries, sorted, rinsed, and patted dry with paper towels

Position the rack in the center of the oven, and preheat the oven to 375°. Coat a muffin pan with cooking spray, and set aside.

To prepare the batter: Combine the flours, baking powder, baking soda, salt, bran, oats, wheat germ, and 1/2 cup of the brown sugar in a large bowl. Mix together with a whisk until blended. Whisk together the eggs, rice milk, margarine, and lemon juice in a small bowl until well blended. Stir the egg mixture into the flour mixture until just combined. Gently fold in the blueberries until incorporated, taking care not to overmix the batter. The batter should look lumpy.

To bake the muffins: Spoon the batter into the prepared muffin tins, filling each cup two-thirds full, and sprinkle with the remaining 1/4 cup brown sugar. Any cups that are not filled with batter should be filled halfway with water to allow for even baking. Bake the muffins until golden brown and a tester inserted in the middle comes out clean, about 20 minutes. Remove the pan from the oven and let cool for about 5 minutes and serve warm. Transfer the muffins to a wire rack and cool completely before storing them in an airtight container.

Brimming with blueberries, with a moist and slightly chewy texture, these muffins should be served warm from the oven while the juices are still bubbling, for an exceptional breakfast treat. Bran is the outer layer of the wheat berry, while the germ is the inner embryo. Both provide a good source of fiber, complex carbohydrates, vitamins, calcium, and other minerals.

Cranberry Banana Oat Bread

Makes one
9-inch loaf

With its moist, tender crumb and the sweet tang of cranberries, this quick bread is a staple at our Thanksgiving breakfast table. By adding your choice of chopped nuts or any type of dried fruit in place of the cranberries, you can easily adapt this basic recipe to your taste.

$1^1/_4$ cups flour
$3/_4$ cup quick oats
1 tablespoon baking powder
$1/_2$ teaspoon salt
2 large eggs
$1/_3$ cup pareve margarine, melted and cooled

$1/_4$ teaspoon freshly squeezed lemon juice
$1^1/_4$ cups mashed ripe banana pulp (2 large or 3 medium bananas)
$1/_2$ cup sugar
$1/_3$ cup dried cranberries

Preheat the oven to 350°. Lightly grease an $8^1/_2$ by $4^1/_2$ by $2^1/_2$-inch loaf pan with a small amount of pareve margarine.

To prepare the batter: Combine the flour, oats, baking powder, and salt in a small bowl. Mix together with a whisk and set aside. Whisk the eggs and margarine together in a large bowl. Add the lemon juice, banana, sugar, and cranberries, and mix until blended. Gently stir in the flour mixture and mix until just combined. Do not overmix the batter.

To bake the bread: Pour the batter into the prepared loaf pan and bake until lightly browned, 45 to 50 minutes. Allow the bread to cool completely in the pan, about 1 hour. Turn the bread out onto a cutting board and, using a serrated bread knife, slice it into $3/_4$-inch-thick pieces. Store the bread by wrapping each piece in plastic wrap and placing them in an airtight container for up to 5 days, or freeze for up to 2 weeks.

Orange Cornmeal Popovers

^{3}/4 cup flour

^{1}/4 cup yellow cornmeal

1 teaspoon sugar

^{1}/4 teaspoon salt

2 large eggs

1 cup rice or soy milk

1 tablespoon pareve margarine,
    melted and cooled

1 teaspoon chopped orange zest

Position the rack in the center of the oven, and preheat the oven to 400°. Coat a muffin pan or six custard cups with pareve margarine or cooking spray, and set aside.

To prepare the batter: Combine the flour, cornmeal, sugar, and salt in a large bowl. Mix together with a whisk. Add the eggs, rice milk, margarine, and orange zest, and beat with an electric mixer until smooth, about 2 minutes, scraping the bowl occasionally with a rubber spatula. Pour the batter into the prepared muffin cups, filling each cup about half full. Bake until the popovers are richly browned, 35 to 40 minutes. Remove from the pan and serve hot.

These delicate, fragile shells puff as they bake, creating air pockets that can be filled with butter and preserves or with a savory stew. Once the popovers are in the oven, resist the temptation to open the oven door for a peek. As the popovers begin to rise above the lip of the cup, the slightest draft will cause them to fall.

Zucchini Orange Bread

Makes one

9-inch loaf

Fragrant orange zest paired with moist zucchini makes this quick bread a favorite with afternoon tea. The recipe is easy to prepare and is a great way to use up an abundance of zucchini from a summer garden. For a nice surprise, double the recipe and bake it in baby loaf pans to make homemade gifts for family and friends.

1½ cups flour
½ cup sugar
2 teaspoons baking powder
½ teaspoon baking soda
¼ teaspoon salt
2 large eggs
⅓ cup pareve margarine, melted and cooled

1½ cups grated zucchini (2 to 3 zucchini)
⅓ cup vanilla rice milk or vanilla soy milk
1½ tablespoons grated orange zest (about 1 orange)
⅓ cup chopped pecans or walnuts

Preheat the oven to 350°. Lightly grease an 8½ by 4½ by 2½-inch loaf pan with a small amount of pareve margarine.

To prepare the batter: Combine the flour, sugar, baking powder, baking soda, and salt in a small bowl. Mix together with a whisk and set aside.

Whisk the eggs and margarine together in a large bowl. Grate the zucchini onto several layers of paper towels, place additional paper towels on top, and press out any excess moisture. Add the zucchini, rice milk, zest, and nuts to the egg mixture, and stir to blend. Gently stir the flour mixture into the zucchini mixture until just combined, taking care not to overmix the batter.

To bake the bread: Pour the batter into the prepared loaf pan and bake until golden brown and a tester inserted in the center comes out clean, 45 to 50 minutes. Allow the loaf to cool 15 minutes in the pan, then turn it out onto a wire rack to cool completely, about 1 hour. Once cool, place the loaf on a cutting board and, using a serrated bread knife, slice it into 3/4-inch-thick pieces. Store the slices by wrapping each piece in plastic wrap and placing them in an airtight container for up to 5 days, or freeze for up to 2 weeks.

Green Onion–Rosemary Drop Biscuits

Makes 6 to 8 biscuits

2¹/₂ cups flour

2¹/₂ teaspoons baking powder

¹/₂ teaspoon baking soda

¹/₂ teaspoon salt

¹/₂ teaspoon sugar

1 cup chopped green onion, both white and green parts (about 1 bunch)

1 tablespoon minced fresh rosemary

2 large eggs

³/₄ cup rice milk or soy milk

1 tablespoon freshly squeezed lemon juice

Preheat the oven to 425°. Lightly grease a baking sheet with vegetable oil.

◗ **To prepare the dough:** Combine the flour, baking powder, baking soda, salt, sugar, green onion, and rosemary in a large bowl. Mix together with a whisk until blended. In a small bowl, whisk together the eggs, rice milk, and lemon juice. Pour the egg mixture into the flour mixture and stir until just combined. Do not overmix the dough.

◗ **To form and bake the biscuits:** Dip a spring-release ice cream scoop into a cup of warm water, and shake off any excess water. Scoop and pack the dough into the ice cream scoop with a rubber spatula. Release the scoop onto the baking sheet, forming a smooth, dome-shaped biscuit. Repeat with the remaining dough, placing the biscuits about 3 inches apart. Bake until golden brown, 12 to 14 minutes.

These biscuits lend themselves nicely to stews and hearty soups. Deliciously enveloped in rosemary essence, they are tender on the inside and slightly crusty on the outside. For a comforting autumn meal, serve them alongside the Shepherd's Pie (page 86).

Sweet Potato Corn Bread

Moist with just a hint of
sweetness, this corn bread
adds color to the Fourth of
July Party menu (page 5)
and is a great companion
for Blackstrap Beans
(page 98).

1 cup flour
1 cup yellow cornmeal
2 tablespoons sugar
2^{1}/$_{2}$ teaspoons baking powder
^{1}/$_{2}$ teaspoon salt
2 large eggs
1 cup rice milk or soy milk

2^{1}/$_{2}$ tablespoons pareve margarine,
  melted and cooled
1 cup baked, peeled, and mashed
  ruby yam (about 1 medium
  yam)
^{1}/$_{2}$ cup white corn kernels, fresh
  (about 1 ear) or frozen

Preheat the oven to 400°. Lightly grease an 8 by 8 by 2-inch glass baking dish
with a small amount of pareve margarine.

⤶**To prepare the batter:** Combine the flour, cornmeal, sugar, baking powder,
and salt in a large bowl. Mix together with a whisk and set aside.

Whisk the eggs, rice milk, and margarine together in a bowl. Add the yam
and corn, mixing until blended. Pour the egg mixture into the flour mixture
and mix until just combined. Do not overmix, as this can cause the corn bread
to be tough.

⤶**To bake the bread:** Pour the batter into the prepared baking dish and bake
until firm or a toothpick inserted in the center comes out clean, about 30 minutes. Allow the bread to cool slightly in the dish, about 10 minutes. Cut the
bread in the dish and serve warm.

Sweet Endings

Nondairy desserts that taste good? You bet! From updated classics to cookies and ice cream, this section will satisfy the dairy-aholic in all of us. When I developed these recipes, my focus was to satisfy the craving for the delicious desserts you always have to say no to. Now you can say yes to Bread Pudding with Pears and Chocolate (page 141), Pumpkin Cheesecake (page 151), and Toasted Coconut Ice Cream (page 138), without the dairy side effects. Some of the recipes in this section specifically call for soy milk with a total fat content of 5g (5 grams per cup). In developing these recipes, I discovered that these particular desserts benefit from the higher fat content found in soy milk, as opposed to rice milk.

Toasted Coconut Ice Cream

This ice cream is so decadently rich that it's hard to believe that it is made without the use of real cream. The toasted coconut doubles the flavor, contributing to its macaroonlike quality. I prefer to use rice milk in this recipe, since it helps to maintain a crisp white color. For a creamier version, use soy milk with a fat content of 5g per cup, along with 2 whole large eggs. Either way, for the best flavor, serve this ice cream slightly softened, straight from the ice cream maker.

1 cup sweetened shredded or flaked
    coconut
1 cup rice milk
2 teaspoons cornstarch
1 cup sugar

1 large egg
1 large egg white
4 cups canned unsweetened
    coconut milk, well blended

To toast the coconut: Preheat the oven to 325°. Spread the coconut in a thin layer on a rimmed baking sheet and toast it in the middle of the oven, stirring frequently, until lightly golden, about 5 minutes. Set aside to cool.

To make the ice cream: Whisk the rice milk and cornstarch in a large saucepan until blended. Add the sugar and eggs, and cook over medium-low heat, whisking constantly, until the sugar is dissolved and the mixture is slightly thickened, about 8 minutes. Take special care not to boil the custard. Remove from the heat and allow the custard to cool slightly. Whisk the coconut milk and toasted coconut into the custard until well blended.

Transfer the mixture to a large metal bowl. Set the bowl in a basin of ice water and let it stand, stirring occasionally, until cooled to room temperature. Cover and refrigerate for at least 6 hours or overnight, to allow the flavors to develop fully.

Stir the mixture and process the custard in an ice cream maker according to the manufacturer's directions.

To store the ice cream: Transfer it to a plastic container with a tight-fitting lid. Place a piece of plastic wrap on top of the ice cream, cover, and freeze.

Flourless Chocolate Almond Cake

12 ounces bittersweet chocolate,
chopped

3/4 cup pareve margarine, cut into
pieces

6 large eggs, separated

3/4 cup sugar

2 teaspoons pure vanilla extract

7 ounces pure almond paste

1/2 cup pareve margarine, cut into
pieces

8 ounces bittersweet or semisweet
pareve chocolate, finely
chopped

1 1/2 tablespoons corn syrup

1 1/4 cups sliced almonds, toasted
(page 175)

To prepare the cake: Preheat the oven to 350°. Line the bottom of a 9-inch springform pan with parchment paper, and generously grease the paper and sides of the pan with about 1 tablespoon of pareve margarine. Set aside.

Stir the chocolate and margarine in a heavy saucepan over low heat until the mixture is melted and smooth. Remove from the heat and allow the mixture to cool, stirring frequently, until lukewarm.

Using an electric mixer, beat the egg yolks and 6 tablespoons of the sugar in a large bowl until the mixture is thick and pale yellow, about 3 minutes. Fold the chocolate mixture into the egg mixture until just incorporated. Fold in the vanilla and set aside.

Using clean, dry beaters, beat the egg whites in a large bowl until soft peaks form. Gradually add the remaining 6 tablespoons sugar and beat just until stiff but not dry peaks form. Gently fold half of the egg whites into the chocolate mixture to lighten it. Fold in the remaining whites until just incorporated. Pour the batter into the prepared pan and bake until the top cracks and a tester inserted in the center comes out with moist crumbs attached, about 50 minutes. Allow the cake to cool in the pan on a wire rack for about 45 minutes. The cake will fall as it cools.

Gently press down on the crusty top to even out the cake, and remove the sides of the pan. Using the cake pan as a guide, cut out a 9-inch cardboard round and place it on top of the cake. Invert the cake onto the round, gently brush away any large crumbs, and allow it to cool completely. The cake can be prepared 1 day ahead if tightly covered and kept at room temperature.

Don't let the lengthy instructions dissuade you from making this cake. It's actually easier than it looks and is sure to satisfy an intense chocolate craving. Almond paste is extremely simple to work with and can be found in the baking section of your supermarket. This cake keeps exceptionally well, covered at room temperature, and can be made a day ahead of time.

⌒**To finish the cake:** Roll the almond paste between 2 sheets of plastic wrap to a thickness of about $^{1}/8$ inch. Cut out a 9-inch circle, using the bottom of the cake pan as a guide. Place the almond circle atop the cake. Transfer the cake to a wire rack, and place the rack over an extra-large bowl. The bowl will be used to catch the excess chocolate glaze.

⌒**To prepare the glaze and decorate the cake:** Set a small saucepan over low heat and melt the margarine, chocolate, and corn syrup, stirring until smooth. Remove from the heat and cool until the glaze is almost set but still spreadable. Spread with just enough glaze on the sides of the cake to even out any imperfections, taking care not to let any crumbs get into the remaining glaze. Slowly reheat the glaze over low heat until it is smooth and just pourable, but not thin and runny. Pour the remaining glaze into the center of the cake and, working quickly, spread it over the top of the cake and around the sides, working the glaze as little as possible. Allow the glaze to cool slightly. Sprinkle the almonds around the outer edge of the top of the cake, forming a $1^{1}/2$-inch border, and gently press them around the sides of the cake so they adhere to the glaze. Transfer the cake to a platter, and allow the glaze to set for about 30 minutes. Serve at room temperature.

Bread Pudding with Pears and Chocolate

2 tablespoons pareve margarine
6 cups lightly packed day-old
    Italian Pugliese bread or sweet
    French bread, cut into 1-inch
    cubes (1-pound loaf)
2 fresh Bosc pears, cored, peeled,
    and cut lengthwise into about
    16 pieces

$^1/_4$ cup pareve chocolate chips
$^1/_3$ cup firmly packed light brown
    sugar
6 large eggs
$3^1/_2$ cups vanilla rice milk or
    vanilla soy milk
Soy Velvet Whipped Cream (page
    148) for garnish (optional)

It's hard to imagine improving upon an old-fashioned comfort food like bread pudding. This version combines two favorites—pears and chocolate—and uses an Italian country bread called Pugliese and fresh Bosc pears. The result is a moist bread pudding with a soufflé-like texture.

To prepare the pudding: Melt the margarine in a glass baking dish measuring 8 by 11 by 2 inches. Scatter half of the bread cubes evenly over the bottom of the dish. Distribute the pears in a single layer on top of the bread. Sprinkle half of the chocolate and half of the brown sugar evenly over the pears. Scatter the remaining bread and chocolate evenly over the top.

Whisk together the eggs and rice milk in a large bowl until well blended. Slowly pour the egg mixture over the top of the bread. Set the dish aside for about 20 minutes, periodically pushing the bread down lightly with the back of a fork, until the bread has absorbed much of the egg mixture. Sprinkle the remaining brown sugar on top of the bread. While the bread is soaking, preheat the oven to 325°.

To bake the bread pudding: Set the baking dish in a larger pan partially filled with hot water, adding the water to the pan after you have placed it in the oven to minimize spilling. Bake, uncovered, for $1^1/_2$ hours. The custard should be slightly soft in the center and the top crispy. Remove from the oven and allow the pudding to cool for 15 minutes before serving. Serve warm with soy whipped cream.

Lemon Blueberry Tart

Tart yet sweet—the combi-
nation of two of my
favorite flavors makes this
dessert scrumptious after
any meal. The blueberries
remain uncooked, keeping
them fresh and juicy. For
the perfect ending to an
hors d'oeuvres party, try
doubling the recipe to
make small assorted fruit
tartlets (about 24 in all).
Arrange sliced strawber-
ries, apricots, raspberries,
or blackberries atop the
custard, brush with the
glaze, and chill.

Custard

3 large eggs

1 large egg yolk

3 tablespoons freshly squeezed
    lemon juice (1 to 2 lemons)

1 teaspoon cornstarch

$^1/_4$ cup pareve margarine

3 tablespoons flour

$^3/_4$ cup sugar

1 tablespoon chopped lemon zest
    (2 to 3 lemons)

......

Tart Pastry

$1^1/_4$ cups flour

3 tablespoons sugar

7 tablespoons pareve margarine

1 large egg yolk

1 tablespoon rice milk or soy milk

......

Glaze

$^1/_4$ cup sugar

1 tablespoon cornstarch

2 tablespoons water

1 teaspoon freshly squeezed lemon
    juice

2 cups fresh blueberries, sorted,
    rinsed, and patted dry with
    paper towels

⤷**To prepare the custard:** Combine the eggs and egg yolk in a small bowl,
whisk to blend, and set aside. Stir together the lemon juice and cornstarch in
a small cup until dissolved. Set aside. Melt the margarine in a large saucepan
over low heat. Whisking constantly, add the flour and cook until it is incorporated and the roux is bubbling, about 1 minute. Add the sugar, lemon juice mixture, and zest, and stir until the sugar dissolves, about 2 minutes. Add the eggs
and cook until the custard thickens, stirring constantly, about 8 minutes. Do
not allow it to boil. Transfer the custard to a small bowl. Cover with plastic
wrap, pressing it onto the surface of the filling. Refrigerate the filling for 6
hours or overnight.

⤷**To prepare and bake the tart shell:** Combine the flour and sugar in a
medium bowl. Add the margarine and crumble with your fingers until the mixture resembles coarse sand. Whisk the egg yolk and rice milk together in a
small bowl. Add the egg to the flour and mix quickly with your hands until the
dough forms a ball. Do not overwork the dough. Press the dough into the

bottom and up the sides of a 9-inch tart pan with removable bottom. Cover and chill for 30 minutes. While the tart shell is chilling, preheat the oven to 400°.

Line the tart shell with aluminum foil, and fill it with dried beans or pie weights. Bake until the sides are set, about 15 minutes. Remove the foil and the beans. Bake until the shell is a deep golden brown, about 15 minutes. Transfer to a wire rack and cool completely. Cover and keep at room temperature. The shell can be made 1 day ahead.

To prepare the glaze and assemble the tart: Spoon the custard into the cooled shell and smooth it out with a rubber spatula. Combine the sugar, cornstarch, water, and lemon juice in a saucepan over medium-low heat. Cook the mixture, stirring constantly, until it thickens and turns translucent, about 4 minutes. Remove from the heat and allow to cool for 1 minute. Gently stir in the blueberries until they are well coated by the glaze. Immediately transfer the berries to the tart, using a slotted spoon. Refrigerate for at least 1 hour before serving or overnight.

The cornmeal adds a surprising texture to this Italian-inspired torta; the pine nuts and custard make it irresistible. Frequently when we get together with friends, we take pleasure in trying out different recipes on each other. That was the case when we enjoyed this little taste of Italy with our friends the Martins. I served this tart with our afternoon coffee as we sat on the patio overlooking their vineyard in the Napa Valley.

Pine Nut Tart

Custard

3 tablespoons pareve margarine
$^1/_4$ cup flour
$1^1/_4$ cups vanilla rice milk or
   vanilla soy milk

4 large egg yolks, beaten (reserve
   1 of the egg whites)
$^1/_4$ cup sugar

......

Pastry

$1^3/_4$ cups flour
$^3/_4$ cup yellow cornmeal
$^1/_3$ cup sugar
$1^1/_2$ teaspoons baking powder

7 tablespoons pine nuts, toasted
   (page 175)

$^1/_2$ cup pareve margarine
2 large eggs
1 tablespoon vanilla rice milk or
   vanilla soy milk

......

Preheat oven to 350°.

To prepare the custard: Melt the margarine in a heavy saucepan over low heat. Whisking constantly, add the flour and cook until it is incorporated and the roux is bubbling, about 1 minute. Whisk in the rice milk, egg yolks, and sugar. Whisking constantly, cook the custard until it thickens, about 5 minutes, taking care not to boil the custard. Set aside to cool.

To prepare the tart shell: Combine the flour, cornmeal, sugar, and baking powder in a large bowl. Mix together with a whisk until blended. Add the margarine and crumble the mixture through your fingers until it resembles coarse sand. Add the eggs and rice milk and mix quickly with your hands until the dough forms a shaggy ball. Do not overwork the dough.

Divide the dough in half and form each half into a slightly flattened disk. Place each disk between 2 sheets of plastic wrap. Using a rolling pin, roll out one of the disks to form a circle 11 to 12 inches in diameter, periodically lifting and repositioning the plastic wrap over the dough. Remove the top layer of plastic wrap and invert the dough into a 9-inch tart pan with a removable bottom. Gently press the dough into the pan, and discard the plastic. Roll out the remaining disk. Lift the plastic off the top of the dough and sprinkle with 2 tablespoons of the pine nuts. Gently roll the rolling pin over the pine nuts to lightly embed them into the dough. Cover again with plastic wrap, and set aside.

♢**To assemble and bake the tart:** Sprinkle the remaining 5 tablespoons pine nuts on the bottom of the tart shell, pour the custard on top, and smooth it out with a rubber spatula. Carefully lift the remaining dough and place it on top of the filling so that the pine nuts are on top. Crimp the edges all around to create a seal. Remove the excess dough overhanging the top of the pan by rolling the rolling pin across the top. Carefully brush the top with the reserved egg white, being careful not to dislodge the pine nuts. Place the tart on a cookie sheet.

Bake until golden brown, 25 to 30 minutes. Cool on a wire rack and serve at room temperature.

Spiced Apple Tart

**Makes one
9-inch tart**

Simply delicious and easy to assemble, this tart is a family favorite. If you enjoy nuts, add some chopped pecans or almonds, or for a tangy sweet tart, use dried cranberries in place of the currants.

Tart Pastry

1¹/₄ cups flour

1 teaspoon sugar

¹/₂ teaspoon baking powder

6 tablespoons pareve margarine

¹/₄ cup rice milk or soy milk

......

Filling

2 pounds Pippin, Golden
    Delicious, or McIntosh apples
    (4 to 5 medium)

¹/₄ cup dried currants

3 tablespoons sugar

1 teaspoon ground cinnamon

2 tablespoons pareve margarine

Preheat oven to 400°.

↪**To prepare the tart shell:** Combine the flour, sugar, and baking powder in a bowl and mix together with a wire whisk until blended. Add the margarine and crumble the mixture with your fingers until it resembles coarse sand. Add the rice milk and mix quickly with your hands until the dough forms a shaggy ball. Do not overwork the dough.

Form the dough into a slightly flattened disk and place between 2 sheets of plastic wrap. Using a rolling pin, roll out the dough to form a circle 11 to 12 inches in diameter, periodically lifting and repositioning the plastic wrap over the dough. Remove the top layer of plastic wrap and invert the dough into a 9-inch tart pan with a removable bottom. Gently press the dough into the pan and discard the plastic. Remove the excess dough overhanging the top of the pan by rolling your rolling pin across the top. Set aside.

↪**To prepare the filling:** Peel the apples, quarter them, remove the cores, and slice them into ¹/₄-inch wedges. Place the first row of apple slices around the outer edge of the tart shell, forming a circle. Repeat the next row by placing the apples closely against the first. Continue the process until you reach the middle. Distribute the currants evenly on top of the apples. In a small bowl, combine the sugar and cinnamon, and sprinkle it evenly over the top. Cut the margarine into small pieces, and dot the apples with the margarine.

Place the tart on a cookie sheet, and bake for 1 hour. Serve warm or at room temperature. The tart can be made 1 day ahead. Cool completely, cover, and keep at room temperature.

Currant Apple Brandy Rice Cake

Makes one
9-inch cake

$^1/_2$ cup brandy

$^1/_3$ cup dried currants

1 large Granny Smith apple,
    peeled, cored, and diced

1$^1/_2$ cups medium-grain white rice
    or short-grain rice (such as
    arborio)

3 cups vanilla rice milk or vanilla
    soy milk

2 cups rice milk or soy milk

1$^1/_4$ cups sugar

$^1/_4$ teaspoon ground cinnamon

4 large eggs, separated

Soy Velvet Whipped Cream (page
    148), for garnish (optional)

Reminiscent of rice pudding, this soft, moist rice cake is rich and deeply satisfying. With just a hint of brandy, along with the gentle sweetness of apples and currants, it's comfort food at its best.

To prepare the cake: Warm the brandy in a small saucepan over low heat, and stir in the currants and apple. Remove the pan from the heat, and set aside.

Meanwhile, combine the rice, rice milk, $^1/_4$ cup of the sugar, and cinnamon in a large saucepan over medium-high heat. Bring the mixture just to a boil, decrease the heat to low, cover, and simmer, stirring occasionally, until the liquid has been absorbed, about 1 hour.

Line the bottom of a 9-inch springform pan with parchment paper. Place the remaining 1 cup sugar in a small skillet over medium-high heat, reserving 1 tablespoon sugar for later use. Cook the sugar without stirring until it begins to melt, about 2 minutes. Continue cooking, stirring constantly, until the sugar is melted and golden, about 3 minutes. Working quickly, pour the caramel into the prepared pan and tilt to coat the bottom and the sides. Set aside to cool.

Preheat the oven to 375°. Strain the currants and apples, using a fine sieve, and discard the brandy. Stir the egg yolks, currants, and apple into the rice mixture until blended. Beat the egg whites in a bowl until foamy. Add the reserved 1 tablespoon of sugar, and continue to beat until soft peaks form. Fold the egg whites into the rice until incorporated. Pour the mixture into the caramelized pan, and set the pan in a larger pan partially filled with water. Bake, uncovered, until golden brown and a knife inserted in the middle comes out clean, about 1 hour. Transfer the cake to a cooling rack and cool to room temperature, about 1 hour. Remove the sides of the pan and place a large platter on the top of the cake. Invert the cake onto the platter, and peel away the parchment paper.

Marble Pound Cake with Strawberries and Cream

Not your typical strawberry shortcake made with a biscuit, this version uses a moist pound cake as the base and is embellished with berries and cream. The unexpected two-tone coloration, as well as the chocolate and strawberry combination, are sure to please both kids and adults alike. At the height of summer—when the strawberries are at their sweetest—tossing them with sugar may not be necessary. If you do elect to use sugar, start with a teaspoon and take it from there. When covered and kept at room temperature, this cake will keep moist for days.

Cake

1 cup pareve margarine at room
    temperature

1²/₃ cups sugar, plus 1 tablespoon

4 large eggs

6 ounces (³/₄ cup) silken soft tofu

1 tablespoon pure vanilla extract

1¹/₂ cups flour

1 teaspoon baking powder

¹/₂ teaspoon salt

¹/₄ cup unsweetened cocoa powder

......

Strawberries

6 cups fresh strawberries, hulled
    and halved

Light brown sugar for tossing with
    berries (optional)

......

Soy Velvet Whipped Cream
(Makes 1³/₄ cups)

1 (10.5-ounce) package firm silken
    tofu

¹/₄ cup rice milk or soy milk

¹/₄ cup confectioners' sugar

2 tablespoons pure maple syrup

2 teaspoons pure vanilla extract

Preheat the oven to 325°. Lightly grease an 8¹/₂ by 4¹/₂ by 2¹/₂-inch loaf pan with a small amount of pareve margarine, and dust with flour. Set aside.

☞**To prepare the cake:** Using an electric mixer, beat the margarine and 1²/₃ cups sugar in a large bowl until creamy, about 1 minute. Add the eggs, one at a time, beating well after each addition. Beat in the tofu and vanilla until the mixture is velvety smooth, about 3 minutes.

Combine the flour, baking powder, and salt in a bowl. Mix together with a whisk until blended. In 2 additions, add the flour mixture alternately with the egg mixture, beating until just combined after each addition and scraping down the sides of the bowl. Transfer two-thirds of the batter to the prepared pan, reserving the rest (about 1¹/₄ cups) in a small bowl. To the reserved batter, add the cocoa powder and the remaining 1 tablespoon sugar, beating well until incorporated. Pour the chocolate batter directly on top of the vanilla batter, in the center and down the length of the pan. Run a small knife through the batters in a swirling pattern to create a marble effect, taking special care not to overswirl the batters.

Bake the cake until golden brown and a tester inserted into the center comes out clean, about $1^1/_2$ hours. Cool the cake in the pan on a wire rack for 20 minutes. Invert the cake onto a rack and cool completely. Wrap the cake in plastic wrap and allow it to stand at room temperature for 1 day.

To prepare the strawberries: Place the strawberries in a bowl and toss with the brown sugar to taste. Marinate until juices form, about 30 minutes and up to 2 hours.

To prepare the whipped cream: Place the tofu, rice milk, sugar, maple syrup, and vanilla in a blender. Whirl at top speed, scraping down the sides often, until smooth about 2 minutes. Transfer the cream to a container with a tight-fitting lid and refrigerate for 1 hour or for up to 3 days. Stir to blend before using.

To assemble the dessert: Slice the cake into $^3/_4$-inch-thick slices, and place the slices on individual dessert plates. Divide the strawberries and their juices equally over the cake slices, and top with the cream.

Rum Caramel Flan

This distinctive custard is delicate and light, kissed with a hint of rum, and makes an elegant dessert. For Valentine's Day, I bake the flan in heart-shaped ramekins, turn the dessert out onto white plates, and garnish each with fresh raspberries.

Caramelized Sugar

$^2/_3$ cup sugar

5 tablespoons water

1 tablespoon dark rum

......

Custard

2 cups soy milk, with total fat of 5g per cup

1 teaspoon cornstarch

$^1/_4$ cup sugar

4 large egg yolks

2 large eggs

$^1/_2$ teaspoon pure vanilla extract

1 tablespoon dark rum

To caramelize the sugar: Arrange six $^3/_4$-cup ramekins or custard cups in a 13 by 9 by 2-inch baking dish. Combine the sugar and water in a small sauté pan over medium-high heat, and cook, stirring constantly, until the sugar has dissolved and the syrup turns a golden color, 2 to 3 minutes. Add the rum and cook for about 30 seconds. Remove from the heat, and immediately pour the syrup into the ramekins, dividing it equally. If the syrup begins to harden before you have finished, return the pan to the heat and stir until it liquefies.

To prepare the custard: Preheat the oven to 350°. Combine the soy milk, cornstarch, and sugar in a heavy medium saucepan. Stir over medium-low heat, until the mixture is warm and the sugar has dissolved, 2 to 3 minutes. Remove from the heat. Whisk the egg yolks and eggs in a medium bowl to blend. Gradually whisk in the warm milk, vanilla, and rum. Divide the mixture equally among the ramekins. Pour enough hot water into the baking dish to come halfway up the sides of the ramekins, being careful not to get any water in the custard mixture. Cover with aluminum foil and bake the custards until the center moves slightly when shaken, about 35 minutes. Remove from the pan and place on a wire rack to cool for about 1 hour. Cover with plastic wrap and chill at least 4 hours or overnight.

To serve, loosen the sides of each flan by running a thin, sharp knife around the edge. Cover the cup with a rimmed dessert plate and, holding both together, quickly invert. Remove the ramekin and serve.

Pumpkin Cheesecake

Makes one

9-inch cake

¹/₄ cup graham cracker crumbs

32 ounces firm tofu, drained

1¹/₂ cups sugar

5 large eggs

¹/₃ cup flour

¹/₄ teaspoon salt

*1 (15-ounce) can solid-pack
    pumpkin purée*

5 teaspoons pumpkin pie spice

*Soy Velvet Whipped Cream (page
    148) for garnish (optional)*

To prepare the pan: Preheat the oven to 325°. Using pareve margarine, thoroughly coat the bottom and sides of a 9-inch springform pan. Place the graham cracker crumbs in the pan and shake to coat the bottom and sides, leaving the excess on the bottom of the pan; set aside.

To prepare and bake the cheesecake: In a large bowl, beat the tofu until creamy. Beat in the sugar gradually. Add the eggs, one at a time, beating well after each addition. Add the flour, salt, pumpkin, and pie spice. Pour the mixture into the prepared springform pan.

Bake until firm, about 1¹/₂ hours. Turn off the heat. The top of the cake will have cracked during baking. Open the oven door slightly and let the cake cool for 30 minutes in the oven. Cool completely on a wire rack, about 2 hours. Remove the sides of the pan, cover, and refrigerate. Before serving, allow the cheesecake to return to room temperature. Garnish each slice with soy whipped cream.

This cheesecake is so rich, creamy, and flavorful, it's hard to believe it is dairy-free. Making it a day ahead allows the cake to settle, giving it a dense texture like that of a dairy cheesecake, but without all the fat.

Need a quick cookie fix? By making the cookie dough in advance and freezing the unsliced logs, you can have fresh-baked chocolate cookies with a tall cold glass of rice or soy milk in just minutes.

Chocolate Mint Cookies

Cookie Dough

2 cups flour

$^3/_4$ cup unsweetened cocoa powder

1 teaspoon baking powder

$^1/_2$ teaspoon baking soda

$^1/_8$ teaspoon salt

$^3/_4$ cup pareve margarine, at room
  temperature

1 cup sugar

1 large egg

$^1/_2$ teaspoon vanilla extract

$^1/_4$ cup rice milk or soy milk

......

Decorator Dough

2 tablespoons pareve margarine, at
  room temperature

2 tablespoons sugar

3 tablespoons rice milk or soy milk

$^1/_2$ cup plus 2 tablespoons flour

$^1/_2$ teaspoon peppermint extract

2 drops green food coloring
  (optional)

To prepare the cookie dough: Combine the flour, cocoa, baking powder, baking soda, and salt in a small bowl. Mix together with a wire whisk and set aside.

Using an electric mixer set at medium speed, cream together the margarine and sugar in a large bowl until fluffy. Add the egg and vanilla, and beat until smooth. Add the flour mixture along with the rice milk, and stir with a large spoon to blend. Divide the dough in half and shape by hand into two 10-inch-long logs, $1^1/_2$ inches in diameter. Tightly wrap each of the logs in plastic wrap and chill in the freezer for 2 hours or overnight. To keep the logs from flattening out on the freezer shelf, insert each of them in a tall glass, or use the cardboard core from a paper towel roll. The dough can be frozen for up to 2 months.

To prepare the decorator dough: Using an electric mixer set at medium speed, cream together the margarine and sugar. Add the rice milk, flour, peppermint extract, and food coloring, and beat until creamy.

To decorate and bake the cookies: Preheat the oven to 325°. Unwrap the frozen logs, and slice with a thin, sharp knife into $^1/_4$-inch-thick rounds. Place the slices on an insulated baking sheet about 2 inches apart. Place the decorator dough in a pastry bag fitted with a size 4 round metal tip. Pipe the dough in various decorative patterns atop each cookie. Suggested designs to use are stripes, dots, zigzags, spirals, and stars. Bake the cookies until they puff slightly, 10 to 12 minutes. Remove the cookies from the oven and allow to cool on the baking sheet for 10 minutes. Using a spatula, transfer the cookies to wire racks and allow to cool completely.

☙**To store the cookies:** Place the fully cooled cookies in an airtight container separated by plastic wrap for up to 1 week, or freeze to store them longer.

Chocolate Chip Macadamia Nut Cookies

I've created a nondairy version of this classic cookie, and it is so good only you will know that it is dairy-free. Adults and kids alike will devour these drop cookies in no time, so be sure to put away a few for yourself.

$2^1/_4$ cups flour

1 teaspoon baking soda

$^1/_2$ teaspoon salt

1 cup pareve margarine, at room temperature

$^3/_4$ cup granulated sugar

$^3/_4$ cup firmly packed light brown sugar

1 teaspoon vanilla extract

2 large eggs

1 (10- to 12-ounce) package pareve chocolate chips

1 cup unsalted macadamia nuts, halved

Preheat the oven to 375°.

To prepare the dough: Combine the flour, baking soda, and salt in a small bowl. Mix together with a wire whisk and set aside.

Using an electric mixer set on medium speed, cream together the margarine, sugars, and vanilla in a large bowl. Add the eggs and continue to mix until incorporated, about 2 minutes. Using a large spoon, stir the flour mixture into the creamed mixture to blend. Add the chocolate and nuts, stirring until incorporated.

To bake the cookies: Place well-rounded teaspoonfuls of dough on a baking sheet about 2 inches apart and bake until light brown, 10 to 12 minutes. Remove the cookies from the oven and allow them to cool on the baking sheet for about 2 minutes. Using a spatula, remove the cookies from the baking sheet and allow to cool completely on wire racks.

To store the cookies: Place the fully cooled cookies in an airtight container for up to 1 week, or freeze to store them longer.

Almond Chocolate Biscotti

2¹/₂ cups flour

2 teaspoons baking powder

¹/₄ cup unsweetened cocoa powder

¹/₂ cup sliced almonds, toasted
    (page 175)

3 tablespoons pareve margarine, at
    room temperature

1 cup sugar

1¹/₂ teaspoons almond extract

3 large eggs

Position a rack in the center of the oven and preheat the oven to 325°.

To prepare the dough: Combine the flour, baking powder, and cocoa, in a bowl, and mix together with a whisk until well blended. Add the almonds and stir to incorporate.

Using an electric mixer, cream together the margarine, sugar, and almond extract at medium speed in a large bowl. Add the eggs, and continue to beat until smooth, about 2 minutes. Using a large spoon, stir the flour mixture into the creamed mixture until just combined. Turn the dough out onto a lightly floured surface. With floured hands, shape the dough into a log approximately 13 inches long by 2¹/₂ inches wide, and 1 inch in diameter.

To bake the biscotti: Line an insulated baking sheet with parchment paper. Transfer the log to the prepared baking sheet. Gently flatten and reshape the log, so that it finishes at about 14 inches long by 3 inches wide and ³/₄ inch high. Bake the log until it is dry and slightly firm to the touch, 30 to 35 minutes. Remove the pan from the oven and decrease the oven temperature to 275°. Allow the log to cool on the pan for about 15 minutes.

Carefully transfer the log to a cutting board, peel away the parchment paper, and discard. With a serrated knife and using a sawing motion, cut the log into ³/₄-inch-thick slices. Place the slices on the same baking sheet, cut side down, and bake until dry and crisp, 30 to 35 minutes. Remove the biscotti from the oven and allow them to cool completely, about 1¹/₂ hours. The biscotti will continue to harden as they cool.

To store the cookies: Place the fully cooled cookies in an airtight container. They will keep for up to 1 week.

Biscotti are classic Italian twice-baked cookies, and what most consider the ultimate dunking cookies for hot coffee. The first time I encountered biscotti, I was twenty years old with a backpack on my back, traipsing around the Tuscan countryside. I remember resting at a streetside café and watching people dunk something in their coffee. I ordered the same and fell in love at first bite.

The origin of these cookies is anyone's guess, as they have been known to be called Mexican wedding cake cookies, Russian tea cookies, and Slavic nut cookies. I've adapted this classic recipe to a nondairy version—the result is, quite simply, delicious.

Tea Cakes

¹/₂ cup pareve margarine, at room temperature
¹/₄ cup granulated sugar
¹/₈ teaspoon salt
1 teaspoon pure vanilla extract

1 cup finely chopped pecans or walnuts
1 cup flour
¹/₂ cup confectioners' sugar

Preheat the oven to 325°.

⌒**To prepare the dough:** Using a hand mixer set on low speed, cream together the margarine, granulated sugar, salt, and vanilla in a large bowl. Add the nuts and flour, mixing until incorporated. Spoon about 1 tablespoon of the dough into the palm of your hand and roll it into a round ball about 1 inch in diameter. Repeat with the remaining dough.

⌒**To bake the cookies:** Place the dough balls on a nonstick baking sheet, about 2 inches apart, and bake until light brown, 20 to 25 minutes. Remove from the oven and cool completely on the baking sheet, about 1¹/₂ hours.

⌒**To coat the cookies:** Place the confectioners' sugar in a quart-size or larger plastic bag. Add the cookies, 6 at a time, to the bag and shake gently to coat. Transfer the cookies to a plate and continue with the next 6 cookies until they have all been thoroughly coated.

⌒**To store the cookies:** Place the fully cooled cookies in an airtight container for up to 1 week, separating them with a layer of plastic wrap, or freeze to store them longer.

Bird's Nest Cookies

Makes 18 to 24 cookies

1/2 cup pareve margarine, at room
   temperature
1/4 cup firmly packed light brown
   sugar
1 large egg, separated
1/8 teaspoon salt

1 teaspoon pure vanilla extract
1 cup flour
3/4 cup finely chopped pecans or
   walnuts
1/4 cup fruit preserves

Preheat the oven to 350°.

Using a hand mixer set on low speed, cream together the margarine, sugar, egg yolk, salt, and vanilla in a large bowl. Add the flour and stir until incorporated.

In a small bowl, beat the egg white to blend. In another small bowl, place the chopped nuts.

To shape and bake the cookies: Spoon about 1 tablespoon of the dough into the palm of your hand and roll it into a round ball about 1 1/2-inches in diameter. Dip the ball into the egg white to coat, and then place it in the nuts, turning to coat. Repeat with the remaining dough. Set the balls on an insulated baking sheet, about 1 inch apart. Gently press your thumb in the center of each ball, creating a well. Spoon 1/2 teaspoon preserves in the hollow of each cookie. Bake until set, 12 to 14 minutes. Remove the cookies from the oven and cool for about 5 minutes on the baking sheet. Using a wide spatula, transfer the cookies to a wire rack, and cool completely.

To store the cookies: Place the fully cooled cookies in an airtight container for up to 1 week, separating them with a layer of plastic wrap, or freeze to store them longer.

I grew up calling these tasty little wonders bird's nests, yet many others know them as thumbprint cookies. Fill them with your favorite preserves or with an assortment of preserves. Either way, they make a colorful addition to a cookie platter.

Ginger Cookies

These delectable cookies are surprisingly moist and rich, with a zippy ginger zing. Try eating them warm from the oven with an icy cold glass of rice milk. They're also wonderful chopped up and sprinkled over a baked apple or poached pears.

2 cups flour

2 teaspoons baking soda

1 tablespoon ground ginger

1 teaspoon ground cinnamon

$^1/_4$ teaspoon ground nutmeg

$^1/_4$ teaspoon ground cloves

$^1/_2$ cup pareve margarine, at room temperature

$^3/_4$ cup firmly packed light brown sugar

1 large egg

$^1/_4$ cup light molasses

2 tablespoons plus $^1/_4$ cup granulated sugar

3 tablespoons crystallized ginger

Preheat the oven to 350°.

To make the dough: Combine the flour, baking soda, ginger, cinnamon, nutmeg, and cloves in a small bowl. Mix together with a whisk until blended. Set aside.

Using an electric mixer set on medium speed, cream together the margarine and brown sugar in a large bowl. Add the egg and molasses, beating until incorporated.

Place 2 tablespoons of the granulated sugar and the crystallized ginger on a cutting board. Coarsely chop the two together, periodically mixing in the sugar to prevent the ginger from sticking to the knife. Add the chopped ginger to the egg mixture and stir to blend. Add the flour mixture to the egg mixture, one-third at a time, and stir with a large spoon until the dough forms a ball. Cover the dough with plastic wrap and refrigerate until firm to the touch, about 1 hour.

To shape and bake the cookies: Spoon about 1 tablespoon of the dough into the palm of your hand and roll it into a round ball about 1 inch in diameter. In a small bowl, place the remaining $^1/_4$ cup sugar and roll the ball in the sugar to coat it. Repeat with the remaining dough. Place the balls on an insulated baking sheet, about 2 inches apart, and bake for 10 to 12 minutes. Watch the cookies carefully; overbaking them will make them dry and hard. Remove the cookies from the oven and cool completely on the baking sheet.

To store the cookies: Place the fully cooled cookies in an airtight container for up to 1 week, or freeze to store them longer.

Oatmeal Almond Lace Cookies

Makes 5 dozen
2¹/₂-inch cookies

1 cup quick oats
¹/₄ cup flour
2 tablespoons finely minced almonds
1¹/₂ teaspoons baking powder
¹/₄ teaspoon salt

¹/₂ cup pareve margarine, at room temperature
1 cup sugar
1 large egg
1 teaspoon almond extract

Delicate and crisp, these cookies are always the first to go at our family gatherings. They are so thin and delicious, it's impossible to eat just one. Serve them on their own or crumbled on top of soy ice cream. Either way they are sure to be a hit in your house too!

Preheat the oven to 325°. Cut 2 pieces of parchment paper to fit 2 insulated baking sheets. Lightly spray the parchment paper with cooking spray, and set aside.

To prepare the dough: Combine the oats, flour, almonds, baking powder, and salt in a small bowl. Mix together with a wire whisk and set aside.

Using an electric mixer set on medium speed, cream together the margarine and sugar in a large bowl. Add the egg and almond extract, and beat until smooth. Add the oat mixture and beat on low speed until just combined.

To bake the cookies: Drop the cookie dough by small teaspoonfuls onto a baking sheet, about 4 inches apart, and bake until edges begin to turn golden brown, 12 to 14 minutes. Remove the baking sheet from the oven and slide the parchment onto the counter. Allow the cookies to cool for about 5 minutes. Using your fingers, peel the cookies off the parchment paper and transfer to a wire rack. Reuse the parchment paper, spraying it with cooking spray between batches. Because these cookies are so thin, they can burn quickly, so watch the time carefully.

To store the cookies: Use plastic wrap to help cushion the cookies, and place them in a sturdy, airtight container for up to 1 week, or freeze to store them longer.

Soy Nog Ice Cream

This rich ice cream is reminiscent of the luscious, sweet flavors of eggnog. Serve it during the holidays with a little brandy drizzled over the top, alongside Ginger Cookies (page 158) or with a sprinkling of chopped Candied Pecans (page 176).

3 large egg yolks
1 large egg
$1^1/4$ cups vanilla soy milk, with
    total fat of 5g per cup

1 cup sugar
$^1/8$ teaspoon ground nutmeg

To prepare the ice cream: Combine the egg yolks, egg, soy milk, sugar, and nutmeg in a large saucepan over medium-low heat, and whisk to blend. Cook, whisking constantly, until the sugar is dissolved and the mixture is slightly thickened, about 8 minutes. Take special care not to boil the custard. Remove the pan from the heat and allow the custard to cool slightly.

Transfer the mixture to a large metal bowl. Set the bowl in a basin of ice water and let stand, stirring occasionally, until cooled to room temperature. Cover and refrigerate for at least 6 hours or overnight, to allow the flavors to develop fully.

Stir the mixture and process the custard in an ice cream maker according to the manufacturer's directions.

To store the ice cream: Transfer it to a plastic container with a tight-fitting lid. Place a piece of plastic wrap on top of the ice cream, cover, and freeze.

Holiday Marzipan Cookies

$^1/_2$ cup pareve margarine, at
    room temperature
$^1/_4$ cup sugar
$^1/_4$ teaspoon almond extract

$1^1/_4$ cups flour
Food coloring in assorted colors:
    red, yellow, green, and blue

↺**To prepare and color the dough:** With the back of a fork, cream together the margarine, sugar, and almond extract. Add the flour, and then, using your hands, mix the dough together thoroughly until it forms a ball. Divide the dough equally among 4 small bowls and cover with plastic wrap until you're ready to mix in the food coloring. Add food coloring to each bowl as instructed below. Using your hands, press and knead the coloring into the dough until it is uniform in color. Cover with plastic wrap until ready to use.

↺**For yellow dough:** Add 4 to 6 drops of yellow food coloring.

↺**To make a banana:** Roll some yellow dough in the palm of your hand into a slightly thick strip. Curve the strip and taper the ends into a banana shape. Flatten the top end slightly, painting the stem and stripe markings on with brown food coloring.

↺**To make a pear:** Roll a 1-inch ball of yellow dough in the palm of your hand. Using your fingers, pinch the top of the ball and curve it slightly, and flatten out the bottom until it resembles a pear shape. Insert a whole clove in the top for the stem. Paint the pear markings using brown coloring.

↺**For green dough:** Add 6 to 8 drops of green food coloring.

↺**To make peas in a pod:** Roll some green dough into a fat strip. Hold the strip in the palm of your hand and, using your pinky, indent the center, building up the sides and pinching the ends (so it resembles a canoe). Roll 3 very small balls and place them inside the pod, gently pinching the sides around each pea. Note: Save a small amount of green dough to use for watermelon rind and carrot and strawberry tops.

↺**For red dough:** Add 6 to 8 drops of red food coloring.

↺**To make a watermelon slice:** Shape some red dough into a flat circle, about $1^1/_2$ inches in diameter and $^1/_4$ inch thick, resembling a large coin. Using a sharp knife, cut it in half to form two half circles. Take a small amount of green dough and roll it into two narrow strips. Shape each of the strips around the

My aunt started a wonderful holiday tradition by gathering all of the children in our family to mold and shape these colorful cookies. I've given directions for making some basic fruit shapes, but don't stop there—let your imagination go wild! Rather than doubling this recipe, I recommend making the basic dough twice; it's much easier to work with that way. Throughout the preparation you will be working and shaping the dough in the palm of your hand and then transferring your cookie to the baking sheet for final shaping and the finishing touches.

curved side of the two half circles and lightly press it into place, forming the watermelon rind. Using brown food coloring, dot the red half circles to resemble seeds.

⌒ **To make a strawberry:** Roll some red dough into a 1-inch ball and, using your fingers, gently pinch the end of the ball and flatten the top slightly in the palm of your hand, creating a strawberry shape. Take a small amount of green dough and roll 2 small, thin strips in the palm of your hand. Place the strips on top of the strawberry in the shape of an X. Using a toothpick, gently prick the strawberry to resemble seeds.

⌒ **For orange dough:** Add 6 drops of red and 4 drops of yellow food coloring.

⌒ **To make a carrot:** In the palm of your hand, roll some orange dough into a 1-inch ball. Continue rolling the dough, elongating it slightly so that it resembles a carrot shape, slightly fatter at the top and thinner at the bottom. Take a very small amount of green dough and roll it into a ball. Pinch the sides to look like a stem, and gently push it into place on top of the carrot. Using the flat side of a toothpick, press down gently in diagonal lines to mark the carrot.

⌒ **To make brown food coloring:** In a shot glass, mix $1/8$ teaspoon water with 3 drops of red, 2 drops of yellow, 1 drop of blue food coloring. To paint markings, use a cotton swab dipped in brown food coloring to brush or dot the appropriate effect.

Place the prepared cookies on an ungreased insulated baking sheet and chill thoroughly in the refrigerator for $1^1/2$ hours.

⌒ **To bake and store the cookies:** Preheat the oven to 300°. Bake for 25 to 30 minutes (the time will vary with the size of the cookies). They will flatten out slightly when baked. Watch carefully, and do not let them brown. Allow the cookies to cool on the baking sheet for 10 minutes, and then transfer them carefully to wire racks. Cool completely before storing.

⌒ **To store the cookies:** Place the fully cooled cookies in an airtight container, separated by plastic wrap, for up to 1 week, or freeze to store them longer.

Basics

The basic recipes in this chapter are the backbone of many of the recipes included in this book. From fresh and flavorful stocks, sauces, and beans to grilled vegetables, toasted breads, and nuts, all of the recipes here are surprisingly uncomplicated to prepare and add superior flavor to any dish. Several of the basic recipes, such as the chicken stock (page 164), vegetable stock (page 165), chopped tomatoes (page 166), and herbed tomato sauce (page 167) freeze nicely, making them convenient for later use. Other recipes offer dairy-free alternatives to commercially prepared products that typically contain dairy, such as the bread crumbs (page 174), toasted breads (page 173), and candied pecans (page 176).

Chicken Stock

Vegetable Stock

Chopped Tomatoes

Herbed Tomato Sauce

Saffron Roasted Garlic

Roasting Peppers

Cooking Beans and Legumes

Grilled Vegetables

Grilled Fruit

Toasted Breads

Bread Crumbs

Toasting Nuts and Seeds

Candied Pecans

Chicken Stock

Makes 8 to 10
cups

Making your own chicken stock is easy and well worth the effort. The next time you roast or grill a chicken, save the bones, wing tips, back, and neck, and store them in a large plastic freezer bag in the freezer. When you have collected 4 pounds' worth, you're ready to make homemade chicken stock. Commercially canned chicken stock can have high amounts of sodium, which can make many dishes too salty. If using canned chicken stock, select one that has reduced sodium and fat. Experiment until you find a brand that suits your taste.

4 pounds chicken bones, wing tips, backs, and necks

2 carrots, peeled, trimmed, and cut into 2-inch pieces

3 stalks celery with leaves, quartered

1 large onion, quartered

8 sprigs flat-leaf parsley, ends trimmed

3 sprigs thyme

1 bay leaf

3 whole black peppercorns

To prepare the stock: Combine the chicken bones, carrots, celery, and onion, in a large stockpot. Add water to cover everything and bring to a rapid boil over high heat; skim off and discard any foam that rises to the top. Decrease the heat to low and add the parsley, thyme, bay leaf, and peppercorns. Simmer, partially covered, for 3 to 4 hours, or until reduced by half, periodically skimming off any residue that rises to the top.

Remove the pot from the heat and strain the stock into a large nonmetallic bowl. Allow the stock to cool, uncovered, at room temperature for about 1 hour.

When cool, cover the stock with plastic wrap and place in the refrigerator for about 2 hours, or until the fat solidifies and rises to the surface. Using a large, flat spoon, remove and discard the fat. The stock is now ready for use, or it can be frozen and stored for later.

To further clarify the stock: Place the refrigerated stock in a large pot and reheat until the stock has just liquefied and is no longer in a gelatinous state, 2 to 3 minutes. Line a fine mesh strainer with cheesecloth. Place the strainer over a clean bowl, and slowly pour the stock into the strainer, eliminating any sediment and peppercorns.

Storage tips: Pour the cooled stock into ice-cube trays and freeze. When the stock has frozen solid, unmold the trays and distribute the cubes among plastic freezer bags. Place the bags back into the freezer for use as needed. The stock will keep, covered, in the refrigerator for up to 3 days or in the freezer for 2 to 3 months.

Vegetable Stock

4 carrots, peeled, trimmed, and
   cut into 2-inch pieces
1 leek top (dark green part only),
   chopped
1 large turnip, trimmed and cut
   into 2-inch pieces
1 large russet potato, peeled, and
   cut into 2-inch pieces
3 stalks celery with leaves,
   quartered

2 large onions, quartered
2 cloves garlic, unpeeled, crushed
   with the side of a knife blade
6 sprigs flat-leaf parsley, ends
   trimmed
4 sprigs thyme
2 sprigs oregano or marjoram
2 bay leaves
8 whole black peppercorns

This is a full-bodied stock prepared entirely from fresh vegetables and takes less time to cook than stocks made from meat. It can be substituted for chicken stock when you need to turn a vegetable-based recipe into a vegan one.

To prepare the stock: Combine the carrots, leek, turnip, potato, celery, onion, and garlic in a large stockpot. Add enough water to cover everything by 2 inches (about 10 cups). Bring to a rapid boil over high heat. Decrease the heat to low, and add the parsley, thyme, oregano, bay leaves, and peppercorns. Simmer, uncovered, for 1^{1}/$_{2}$ hours. Line a fine-mesh strainer with cheesecloth. Place the strainer over a clean bowl and slowly pour the stock into the strainer, eliminating any sediment and peppercorns. With the back of a large spoon, lightly press on the vegetables to extract as much liquid as possible, then discard the vegetables.

Storage tips: Pour the cooled stock into ice-cube trays and freeze. When the stock has frozen solid, unmold the trays and distribute the cubes among plastic freezer bags. Place the bags back into the freezer for use as needed. The stock will keep, covered, in the refrigerator for up to 3 days or in the freezer for 2 to 3 months.

Chopped Tomatoes

Used as a base in many recipes, these skinned and chopped tomatoes are a flavorful addition to light sauces, soups, and pastas. If desired, try seasoning the tomatoes lightly with salt and pepper and fresh basil, leaving the leaves either whole or finely chopped.

1^1/$_2$ pounds medium-size vine-ripened tomatoes

◠**To prepare the tomatoes:** Fill a large, deep bowl with ice water and set aside. Bring a large pot of water to a boil over high heat. Immerse the tomatoes in the boiling water for 10 to 45 seconds, or until the tomato skin cracks. Using a large slotted spoon, quickly transfer the tomatoes to the ice bath for about 30 seconds. Lift the tomatoes out, allow them to cool briefly, and then pull off and discard the skin. Cut out the cores, coarsely chop the tomatoes, and place them in a large bowl along with their juices, or refrigerate or freeze until ready to use.

Note: These chopped tomatoes freeze beautifully, preserving the taste of summer for enjoyment later in the year. I recommend freezing 1 cup of chopped tomatoes per freezer bag. That way you can use exactly what you need, as you need it. In a pinch, you can use commercially canned tomatoes in place of the fresh; just be sure to purchase ones with no added salt.

Herbed Tomato Sauce

2¹/₂ pounds medium-size vine-
    ripened tomatoes
3 tablespoons olive oil
1 large yellow onion, minced
3 cloves garlic, minced
1 bay leaf
3 sprigs thyme

1 teaspoon salt
¹/₄ teaspoon freshly ground black
    pepper
Sugar, if necessary
¹/₄ cup chopped fresh basil
1 tablespoon minced fresh flat-leaf
    parsley

To prepare the tomatoes: Fill a large, deep bowl with ice water and set aside. Bring a large pot of water to a boil over high heat. Immerse the tomatoes in the boiling water for 10 to 45 seconds or until the tomato skin cracks. Using a large slotted spoon, quickly transfer the tomatoes to the ice bath for about 30 seconds. Lift the tomatoes out, allow them to cool briefly, and then pull off and discard the skin. Cut out the cores, halve the tomatoes horizontally, and squeeze out and discard the juice and seeds. Finely chop the tomatoes.

To make the sauce: Heat the olive oil in a large saucepan over medium-high heat and sauté the onion until softened and slightly browned, about 5 minutes. Stir in the garlic and sauté for 1 minute. Add the tomatoes, bay leaf, thyme, salt, and pepper. Bring to a boil, and decrease the heat to low. Simmer the sauce, uncovered, for 20 to 30 minutes, stirring occasionally. Taste and correct the seasonings. If the sauce is very acidic, add a pinch or two of sugar, or more to taste. The finished sauce will have a slight texture to it. If you prefer a smooth, refined sauce, pass the sauce through a food mill or purée it in a blender. Stir in the basil and parsley. Check the consistency. If you desire a thicker sauce, return it to the saucepan and cook it over medium-low heat until it is as thick as you like. The sauce will thicken as it cools. Transfer the sauce to a non-metallic container with a tight-fitting lid, and refrigerate for up to 5 days.

This basic tomato sauce can be made quickly and with very little effort. Although I often use commercially canned tomatoes for cooking, nothing can compare with fresh summer tomatoes from the garden, with their bright, fresh-tasting flavor. Depending on the size of my tomato crop, I often double or triple this recipe, freezing or canning the extra sauce and enjoying it during the winter months. This sauce can be used anytime tomato sauce is called for. For a change, enliven it with capers, roasted peppers and anchovy.

Saffron Roasted Garlic

Garlic lovers, this one's for
you. Saffron imparts a rich
golden color that makes
these tender roasted
heads of garlic irresistible.
Serve them warm by
squeezing the cloves out
of their skins and spread-
ing them onto crusty
bread.

4 whole heads of garlic (3 to 4
   ounces each)
$^1/_4$ cup extra virgin olive oil

$^1/_2$ teaspoon saffron threads
$^1/_2$ teaspoon salt

To prepare and roast the garlic: Preheat the oven to 325°. Slice the top
$^1/_2$-inch from each of the heads of garlic. Remove some of the papery outer
skin, keeping the heads intact. Place the root ends down in a garlic baker or
close-fitting covered baking dish. Drizzle each head of garlic with 1 tablespoon
olive oil and $^1/_8$ teaspoon salt. Cover the dish and bake for 45 minutes.

Uncover the dish and divide the saffron equally among the heads. Baste
with the oil in the dish. Cover and continue baking until the cloves are very soft
and golden, 30 to 40 minutes.

Roasting Peppers

⤳**To grill bell peppers:** Preheat a grill to 450° (a hot fire). Cut the bell peppers in half lengthwise and remove the stems and seeds. Place them skin side down on the grill, and grill until the skin is charred and bubbled. Turn and continue grilling the inside of the pepper for about 1 minute; do not blacken the inside. Place the peppers in a bowl, cover the bowl with a plate or with plastic wrap, and allow the peppers to steam for about 20 minutes.

⤳**To grill whole peppers, including chiles:** Leave the peppers whole and place them on the hot grill, turning them until the skin is bubbled and completely charred. Place the peppers in a bowl, cover the bowl with a plate or with plastic wrap, and allow the peppers to steam for about 20 minutes.

⤳**To roast peppers on a gas cooktop:** Place whole peppers over a gas flame, turning and watching constantly, until the skin bubbles and is completely charred on all sides. Place the peppers in a bowl, cover the bowl with a plate or with plastic wrap, and allow the peppers to steam for about 20 minutes.

⤳**To roast peppers under a broiler:** Line the top rack of the oven with aluminum foil. Cut the peppers in half lengthwise, and remove the stems and seeds. Place the peppers skin side up under the preheated broiler and broil about 3 inches from the heat source until the skin bubbles and is completely charred. Place the peppers in a bowl, cover the bowl with a plate or with plastic wrap, and allow the peppers to steam for about 20 minutes.

⤳**To clean the peppers:** Remove the charred skin by gently rubbing it off by hand or by lightly scraping it off with a sharp knife. Discard the stems and seeds.

⤳**To store the peppers:** If you won't be using them immediately, cut the roasted, cleaned peppers into long segments and layer them in a dish with olive oil and any reserved juices. Cover the peppers tightly and refrigerate for up to 5 days.

Charred food is generally not the desired result in cooking. However, when you're roasting peppers, charring the skin imparts a wonderful distinctive flavor to the flesh beneath. Here are three different methods that all work equally well, my favorite being the grill/barbecue method.

Dried beans are simple to
prepare and provide thi-
amin, riboflavin, niacin,
iron, and calcium.

Cooking Beans and Legumes

To clean the beans and prepare them for soaking: Place 1 pound of dried beans on a clean, flat surface, preferably light in color to visually aid in the sorting. Sort through the beans and discard any pebbles or chaff. Place the sorted beans in a colander and rinse with cold running water. Dried beans can take a long time to cook unless they have been soaked prior to cooking. You can shorten their cooking time by using one of the following soaking methods.

Quick soaking method: Combine 1 pound dried beans, 1 teaspoon salt, and 6 to 8 cups water in a large stockpot. Bring to a rapid boil over high heat, and boil for about 2 minutes. Remove the pot from the heat, cover tightly, and allow the beans to soak for 1 hour. Drain the soaked beans in a colander and rinse them under warm running water.

Overnight soaking method: Combine 1 pound dried beans, 2 teaspoons salt, and 6 to 8 cups water in a large stockpot. Let the beans soak overnight. Drain the soaked beans in a colander and rinse them under cold running water.

To cook the beans: Combine the rinsed soaked beans, 1 teaspoon salt, and 6 to 8 cups water in a large stockpot. Bring the pot to a rapid boil over high heat, partially cover the pot, and reduce the heat to a gentle, rolling boil. Cook the beans until tender, using the approximate cooking times listed below. Check the beans periodically and add more water if necessary to keep them immersed in water. Drain the beans and use as needed.

Approximate Cooking Times for Soaked Dried Beans

Black beans: 1 to $1^{1}/_{4}$ hours

Garbanzo beans (chickpeas): $2^{1}/_{2}$ to 3 hours

Great Northern, kidney, and pinto beans: $1^{1}/_{2}$ to 2 hours

Lima beans: $^{1}/_{2}$ to 1 hour

White beans (navy beans): 45 minutes to $1^{1}/_{4}$ hours

Lentils and split peas: 1 to $1^{1}/_{2}$ hours (do not soak)

Grilled Vegetables

2 Japanese eggplants, unpeeled,
 ends trimmed and halved
 lengthwise
2 zucchini, unpeeled, ends
 trimmed and halved
 lengthwise
2 yellow crookneck squash,
 unpeeled, ends trimmed and
 halved lengthwise
2 red bell peppers, halved
 lengthwise, seeded, and
 deribbed
3 tablespoons olive oil
1 teaspoon salt
$^1/_2$ teaspoon freshly ground black
 pepper
2 teaspoons garlic powder

To prepare and grill the vegetables: Preheat the grill to 350° (a medium-hot fire). Place the eggplant, zucchini, and yellow squash halves on a cutting board with the cut side facing up. Using a small, sharp knife, score each vegetable half by making 3 to 4 diagonal slits, no more than $^1/_4$ to $^1/_2$ inch deep. Transfer the eggplant, zucchini, yellow squash, and bell pepper, cut side up, to a large shallow roasting pan. Pour the olive oil over the vegetables, and sprinkle with salt, pepper, and garlic powder. Using your hands, rub the oil and seasonings into the vegetables, coating them completely. Place the vegetables on the hot grill, cut side down, and grill for about 6 minutes. Using tongs, turn the vegetables over so that the skin side is on the grill. Grill for about 5 minutes, or until the vegetables are tender. Arrange the grilled vegetables on a platter, cut side up, and serve hot, warm, or cold.

Because the size of the vegetables can vary and different areas of the grill can be hotter than others, watch the grilling closely, and use the suggested cooking times only as a guide.

When making grilled vegetables for a large group, double or triple the recipe, and grill the vegetables until they are well scored but still firm. Arrange them in a shallow roasting pan, cover tightly with aluminum foil, and place the pan in a 200° oven for up to 45 minutes. The slow oven will finish steaming the vegetables and will give you the time you need to set up the rest of the food.

Grilled Fruit

When we installed our gas barbecue, we began grilling everything from appetizers to dessert—the dessert, of course, being fresh fruit. The first fruit we grilled was figs, and they were such a huge success that we've since tried numerous other fruits. Here are a few of our favorites.

Grilled Figs

8 ripe black figs, rinsed and wiped
  dry

To prepare and grill the figs: Preheat the grill to 350° (a medium-hot fire). Cut each fig in half lengthwise. Place them flesh side down on the grill for 2 minutes. Using tongs, turn the figs over so that the skin side is on the grill. Grill until the figs are soft and caramelized, 3 to 4 minutes more. Carefully remove the figs from the grill and place them on a plate, flesh side up. Allow the figs to cool to room temperature before serving, about 5 minutes.

Served alone or as part of a salad, grilled figs make a wonderful starter or accent to the main course.

Grilled Nectarines, Peaches, or
Apricots

4 unpeeled nectarines, peaches, or
  apricots
8 teaspoons light brown sugar

To prepare and grill the fruit: Preheat the grill to 350° (a medium-hot fire). Cut around the fruit down to the pit, following the natural seam. Separate the halves by rotating them in opposite directions, pulling them apart, and removing the pit. Place them flesh side down on the grill for about 3 minutes. Using tongs, turn the fruit over so that the skin side is on the grill. In the hollow left by the pit, sprinkle each half with 1 teaspoon of brown sugar, and grill for about 5 minutes. Carefully remove the fruit from the grill and place on a plate, flesh side up. Allow the fruit to cool slightly, 3 to 4 minutes, before serving.

Choose the freestone varieties for grilling; it makes removing the pit a lot easier.

Toasted Breads

Garlic Pita Crisps

6 (6-inch-diameter) pita breads,
　　plain or onion

$^1/_3$ cup olive oil

4 cloves garlic, minced

$^1/_8$ teaspoon salt

Paprika for sprinkling

To prepare the pita bread: Preheat the oven to 325°. Slice the pita bread in half horizontally, forming 2 separate rounds, 12 in all. Place the inside or rough side of the bread facing up on a cutting board. Combine the olive oil, garlic, and salt in a small bowl, and stir well to blend. Using a pastry brush, lightly brush each of the rounds with the olive oil mixture, using all of the oil. Sprinkle with paprika. Cut each round into 6 equal wedges and arrange on a large baking sheet. You will need to bake them in batches. Bake the pita wedges until they are golden brown and crisp, 10 to 12 minutes. Transfer the wedges to a wire rack, and cool completely.

Herb Toasts

$^1/_2$ cup olive oil

1 tablespoon minced fresh
　　rosemary

1 teaspoon minced fresh thyme

$^1/_4$ teaspoon salt

$^1/_8$ teaspoon freshly ground black
　　pepper

1 baguette, sweet or sourdough,
　　sliced $^1/_4$-inch thick

To prepare the baguette: Preheat the oven to 250°. Combine the olive oil, rosemary, thyme, salt, and pepper in a small saucepan and stir over low heat until fragrant, about 3 minutes. Place the bread rounds on a baking sheet and brush lightly with the olive oil mixture, using all of the oil. Bake the rounds until golden brown and crisp throughout, 20 to 30 minutes. Check on them periodically, as they can burn easily. Transfer the toasts to a wire rack and cool completely.

Although there is a wide assortment of crackers and toasted breads to choose from in the super-market, most contain dairy. Here are two dairy-free alternatives to com-plement your appetizers. Both can be made up to 3 days ahead and stored at room temperature in tightly covered containers or heavy plastic storage bags. It's important to allow the breads to cool completely before storing them or they will become soggy. If this happens, place the bread on a cookie sheet and reheat in a 325° oven for about 5 minutes.

Bread Crumbs

1 pound loaf sweet French bread or
  baguette

⌒**To prepare the bread crumbs:** Preheat the oven to 300°. Slice the bread into $^1/_2$-inch-thick slices and place in a single layer on a baking sheet. Place the sheet in the oven, and bake until the bread is dry but not hard, 15 to 20 minutes. Remove from the oven and cool. Break the slices up with your hands, then grind them in a blender or food processor until the texture ranges from fine to a little coarse.

Trying to find bread crumbs that do not contain dairy is no easy task. Commercially packaged plain or seasoned bread crumbs often contain dairy in the form of whey or dried cheese. Fortunately, making bread crumbs at home is so easy you'll never have to look for them again. I like making mine with sweet French bread, but almost any bread will do, including sourdough and wheat.

Toasting Nuts and Seeds

⊙**To toast nuts:** Place the nuts in a large skillet over medium-high heat. Toss them continuously in the skillet until the nuts begin to crackle and turn a light golden color. Transfer the nuts to a plate and spread them out in a single layer to cool.

⊙**To toast sesame seeds:** Place the seeds in a small skillet over medium-low heat. Toss the seeds continuously in the skillet until they begin to crackle and pop, 1 to 2 minutes. Transfer the seeds to a plate and spread them out in a single layer to cool.

⊙**To roast nuts:** Preheat the oven to 300°. Line the bottom of a rimmed baking sheet with parchment paper. Spread the nuts on the prepared pan in a single layer. Bake for 10 to 15 minutes, depending on the size of the nuts being roasted. Nuts can burn easily, so watch them closely, baking until they turn a light golden color.

⊙**To store toasted or roasted nuts or seeds:** Allow the nuts or seeds to cool completely before you store them, or they will become soggy. Store the nuts and seeds in an airtight container at room temperature for up to 1 week.

Toasting nuts is a delicious way to bring out the crisp texture and full flavor of your favorite nuts. The method described here works equally well for shelled raw almonds, cashews, pine nuts, pecans, walnuts, and macadamia nuts. Nuts retain their heat long after being removed from the cooktop, so it is very important not to overcook them, since they will continue to darken as they cool.

Candied Pecans

These nuts can be used in a variety of ways. They make a nice accompaniment to an hors d'oeuvre table, or they can be tossed into a salad or used as a dessert topping. For a hot and spicy variation, add ^{1}/$_4$ teaspoon cayenne pepper and ^{1}/$_2$ teaspoon each of ground cinnamon, ginger, and allspice to the sugar before adding it to egg whites. If you prefer, use walnuts instead of the pecans.

1 large egg white
^{1}/$_8$ teaspoon salt
^{1}/$_2$ cup sugar

2^1/$_2$ cups shelled pecan halves
(10 ounces)
^{1}/$_4$ cup pareve margarine

To coat the pecans: Using an electric mixer, beat the egg white and salt in a large bowl until foamy. Gradually add the sugar, beating just until blended. Do not overbeat; the mixture should be runny. Add the pecan halves and stir to coat with a rubber spatula.

To bake the pecans: Preheat the oven to 325°. Cut the margarine into 4 pieces and place the pieces on a nonstick rimmed baking sheet. Place the pan in the oven and melt the margarine, taking care not to burn it. Remove the pan from the oven and tilt to coat it evenly with the melted margarine. Spread the pecans on the prepared pan in a single layer, separating any that stick together. Bake for 10 minutes on the first side, and then, using a spatula, turn the pecans over, again separating any that stick together. Continue baking until they turn a rich golden color, 8 to 10 minutes more. Nuts can burn easily, so watch them closely. Total baking time is about 20 minutes.

Remove the pan from the oven and allow the pecans to cool for about 10 minutes. Loosen them with a spatula and cool completely in the pan for about 2 hours.

Cool the pecans completely before storing them, or they will become mushy. Store the pecans in an airtight container at room temperature for up to 1 week.

Bibliography and Resources

Books about Allergies and Nutrition

Brostoff, Jonathan, M.D., and Linda Gamlin. *Food Allergies & Food Intolerance*, 3rd edition. Rochester, VT: Healing Arts Press, 2000.

Carter, Jill, with Alison Edwards. *The Elimination Diet Cookbook*. New York: Element Books, 1997.

Netzer, Corrine T. *The Complete Book of Food Counts*. New York: Dell Publishing, 2000.

Page, Linda. *Healthy Healing*, 11th edition. Carmel Valley, CA: Healthy Healing Publications, 2000.

Ulene, Art. *Nutrition Facts Desk Reference*. New York: Avery Publishing Group, 1995.

Walsh, William E., M.D. *Food Allergies*. New York: John Wiley & Sons, 2000.

Williams, Melvin H. *Nutrition for Fitness & Sport*, 4th edition. New York: McGraw-Hill, 1995.

Cookbooks

Bronfman, Rachelle, and David Bronfman. *CalciYum!* Toronto: Bromedia, 1998.

Kidder, Beth. *The Milk-Free Kitchen*. New York: Henry Holt & Co., 1991.

Lanza, Louis, and Laura Morton. *Totally Dairy-Free Cooking*. New York: William Morrow, 1999.

McCarty, Meredith. *Sweet and Natural*. New York: St. Martin's Press, 1999.

Shurtleff, William, and Akiko Aoyagi. *The Book of Tofu*. Berkeley: Ten Speed Press, 1998.

Zukin, Jane. *Dairy-Free Cookbook*, 2nd edition. Roseville, CA: Prima Publishing, 1998.

Additional Resources/Online Resources

The Food Allergy and Anaphylaxis Network
10400 Eaton Place, Suite 107
Fairfax, VA 22030-2208
800-929-4040
http://www.foodallergy.org

American Academy of Allergy Asthma & Immunology
611 E. Wells Street
Milwaukee, WI 53202
800-822-2762
http://www.aaaai.org

National Osteoporosis Foundation
1232 22nd Street N.W.
Washington, DC 20037-1292
800-223-9994 or 202-223-2226
http://www.nof.org

The Calcium Information Center
1-800-321-2681
http://www.calciuminfo.com

U.S. Soyfoods Directory
5757 W. 74th Street
Indianapolis, IN 46278-1755
http://www.soyfoods.com

Food and Drug Administration (FDA)
Freedom of Information Staff
5600 Fishers Lane, HFI-35
Rockville, MD 20857
888-463-6332
http://www.fda.gov

U.S. Food and Drug Administration
FDA Consumer Magazine
July/August 2001
Volume 35, Number 4
Living With Food Allergies
By Anne Munoz-Furlong

U.S. Department of Agriculture (USDA)
Nutrient Data Laboratory
Agricultural Research Service
Beltsville Human Nutrition Research Center
10300 Baltimore Avenue
Building 005, Room 107, BARC-West
Beltsville, MD 20705-2350
301-504-0630
http://www.nal.usda.gov./fnic/foodcomp

National Dairy Council
10255 West Higgins, Number 900
Rosemont, IL 60018
800-426-8271 or 847-803-2000
http://www.nationaldairycouncil.org

Dairy Council of California
1101 National Drive, Suite B
Sacramento, CA 95834
In CA: 888-868-3133
Outside CA: 888-868-3083
http://www.dairycouncilofca.org

Manufacturers and Distributors

Aidells Sausage Co.
1625 Alvarado Street
San Leandro, CA 94577
877-243-3557
Assorted chicken, turkey, pork, beef,
    and lamb sausage
http://www.aidells.com

Campbell Soup Co.
Consumer Response Center
Campbell Place Box 26B
Camden, NJ 08103-1701
800-442-7684
Swanson chicken and vegetable broth
http://www.swansonbroth.com

**Double Rainbow Gourmet Ice Creams,
    Inc**.
275 South Van Ness Avenue
San Francisco, CA 94103
800-489-3580
Soy cream frozen desserts
http://www.doublerainbow.com

Dreyer's Grand Ice Cream, Inc.
5929 College Avenue
Oakland, CA 94618
877-437-3937
Known as Eddy's east of the Rockies
Assorted sorbet flavors
http://www.dreyers.com

Eden Foods, Inc.
701 Tecumseh Road
Clinton, MI 49236
800-248-0320
Organic products and milk alternatives
http://edenfoods.com

Galaxy Nutritional Foods
2441 Viscount Row
Orlando, FL 32809
800-808-2325
(Soy Co Foods is a division of Galaxy
    Nutritional Foods.)
Milk and cheese alternatives
http://www.galaxyfoods.com

Ghirardelli Chocolate Co.
1111 1139th Avenue
San Leandro, CA 94578-2361
510-483-6970
Baking chocolate
http://www.ghirardelli.com

Grainaissance, Inc.
1580 62nd Street, Emeryville, CA 94608
510-547-7256
Amazake beverages, rice nog, pudding,
    and mochi
http://www.grainaissance.com

Häagen-Dazs
Ice Cream Partners
12647 Alcosta Boulevard, Suite 300
San Ramon, CA 94583
800-767-0120
Assorted sorbets
http://www.haagen-daz.com

**Hain Food Group, Natural Food
    Division**
16007 Camino de la Cantera
Irwindale, CA 91706-7811
800-434-4246
Milk alternatives, soup stock, soy sauce,
    full line of assorted products.
Hain distributes Arrowhead Mills,
    Westsoy, Westbrae, and Health Valley.
Westbrae Natural Foods:
    http://www.westbrae.com

Imagine Foods, Inc.
1245 San Carlos Avenue
San Carlos, CA 94070
650-595-6300
Milk alternatives and frozen desserts
http://www.imaginefoods.com
e-mail: info@imaginefoods.com

Knudsen and Sons, Inc.
37 Speedway Avenue
Chico, CA 95928
530-899-5000
Fruit juices and spreads
http://knudsenjuices.com

Kraft Foods, Inc.
1 Kraft Court
Glenview, IL 60025
800-431-1001
Baker's baking chocolate
http://www.kraftfoods.com

Lipton
800 Sylvan Avenue
Englewood Cliffs, NJ 07632-9976
800-735-3554
Shedd's Willow Run Soybean Margarine
http://www.lipton.com

Lundberg Family Farms
5370 Church Street
Richvale, CA 95974
530-882-4551
Rice and grain products
http://www.lundberg.com

Morinaga Nutritional Foods, Inc.
2050 W. 190th Street, #110
Torrance, CA 90504
800-699-8638
Mori-Nu silken style tofu
http://www.morinu.com

Nancy's, Springfield Creamery
29440 Airport Road
Eugene, OR 97402
541-689-2911
Cultured soy yogurt
http://www.nancysyogurt.com

Odense Marzipan
Andre Prost, Inc.
P.O. Box 835
Old Saybrook, CT 06475
800-243-0897
Pure almond paste
http://www.andreprost.com

Pacific Foods of Oregon, Inc.
19480 SW 97th Avenue
Tualatin, OR 97062
503-692-9666
Milk alternatives, chicken and vegetable
    stock
http://www.pacificfoods.com

**Pepperidge Farm, Inc., a division of
    Campbell Soup Co.**
Campbell Place Box 26B
Camden, NJ 08103-1701
800-762-8301
Frozen puff pastry
http://www.puffpastry.com

Quaker Oats Company
P.O. Box 049003
Chicago, IL 60604-9003
800-367-6287 or 800-407-2247
Oatmeal, Aunt Jemima original pancake
and waffle mix
http://www.quakeroatmeal.com

San-J International, Inc.
2880 Sprouse Drive
Richmond, VA 23231
800-446-5500
Tamari soy sauce
http://www.san-j.com

Trader Joe's
P.O. Box 3270
South Pasadena, CA 91031-6270
626-441-2024 ext. 355
Wide assortment of dairy-free products
http://www.traderjoes.com

Tropical Source—nSpired Natural Foods
San Leandro, CA 94577
Tropical Source chocolate chips
http://www.nspiredfoods.com

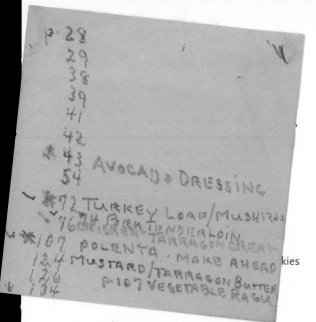

Handwritten note (overlay):
p. 28
29
38
39
41
42
43
54
AVOCADO DRESSING
*72 TURKEY LOAF/MUSHRO
76 ST. PORK TENDERLOIN
TARRAGON CREAM
*107 POLENTA - MAKE AHEAD
124 MUSTARD/TARRAGON BUTTER
126
134   P-107 VEGETABLE RAGU

Vitasoy USA Inc.
400 Oyster Point Boulevard
South San Francisco, CA 94080
800-328-8638
Nasoya tofu, milk alternatives, and
    Azumaya products—wonton wraps
http://www.vitasoy-usa.com

White Wave Inc.
1990 North 57th Court
Boulder, CO 80301
800-488-9283
Silk soymilk creamer, yogurt, and soy
    nog; White Wave tofu and tempeh
http://www.whitewave.com

Whole Foods Market, Inc.
601 North Lamar, Suite 300
Austin, TX 78703
512-477-4455
Natural and organic food supermarkets,
    complete assortment of natural and
    organic foods and beverages,
    including dairy-free products
http://www.wholefoodsmarket.com

WholeSoy Co.
49 Stevenson Street, Suite 1075
San Francisco, CA 94105
415-495-2870
Organic soy yogurt, cultured soy
    beverage, and Glace frozen desserts
http://www.wholesoycom.com

Wild Oats Markets, Inc.
3375 Mitchell Lane
Boulder, CO 80301
800-494-WILD
Natural and organic food supermarkets,
    assortment of dairy-free products

Wildwood Natural Foods
135 Bolinas Road
Fairfax, CA 94930
800-499-8638
Tofu, milk alternatives, and assorted
    tofu products
http://www.wildwoodnaturalfoods.com

Index